POCKET PRECINCTS



# KYOTO

A pocket guide to the city's best cultural hangouts, shops, bars and eateries

STEVE WIDE AND MICHELLE MACKINTOSH

hardie grant books

# CONTENTS

# INTRODUCTION

Maido! Konichiwa! Welcome to Kyoto.

Slip off your shoes, slide on a yukata (casual cotton kimono) and get ready to take life at Kyoto pace. The 'wa' in 'konichiwa' means harmony, peace and balance, which reflects a way of living full of reflection, inspiration and creation. It's a city of tradition and history, where the influence of ancient temples and shrines, with their deep spiritual roots, touches every aspect of daily life. Kyoto is all about the seasons, which is reflected in everything from food, festivals and craft to the intense appreciation of leaves, flowers, moss and snow. It's the artisan capital of Japan. The ancient arts of making tea, lacquerware, ceramics, handmade paper, cooking utensils, fans and textiles are still practised today.

In a country with so much heritage, Kyoto is showing a sensitivity to the past while keeping an eye on the future. New generations are renovating old townhouses, setting up exciting new retail spaces and opening cafes, restaurants and stores with their own take on anything from coffee to handmade paper.

Kyoto is a city surrounded by mountains. It has 2000 temples and shrines, zen gardens and geisha culture, all of which give Kyoto a magical calm. It has beautiful restaurants in centuries-old houses and temples with vegan banquets. You'll also find amazing street food, knockabout izakayas (gastropubs) and ramen joints, sake bars, craft brewers, sweets too beautiful to eat, and regional specialties and flavours that will challenge and delight your senses.

Join us as we navigate Kyoto's ancient pathways, temples, gardens and narrow, lantern-lit alleys to reveal the city's precincts and find out what makes them unique. We'll explore some of the secret treasures, unique shopping and eating opportunities hidden in the streets and lanes. Along the way we'll uncover new Kyoto, a dynamic and evolving city taking the skills and lessons of the past and using them to forge a vibrant and exciting present.

**Steve and Michelle**

# A PERFECT KYOTO DAY

Whenever we arrive in Kyoto, the air is alive with possibilities. Some of our favourite places in the world are in this city, and we can never wait to get started.

Early morning in Kyoto is best spent with the locals, sipping creamy café au lait and munching on egg sandwiches at **Inoda**, or relaxing with a pour-over at cosy **Clamp Coffee Sarasa**. We like to see what Kyoto has been up to – a walk down Shijo-dori (with a purchase or two) and a glimpse of the window displays at **Takashimaya** brings us up to date. From here, we head to chaotic and colourful **Nishiki Market** to shop for kitchenalia, stock up on crackers, pickles and sweets and indulge in a tasting or two. For lunch, we go to the **D&Department Shokudo** on the grounds of **Bukkoji Temple** for a simple and delicious lunch, or grab a picnic hamper from **Wife and Husband** to take into the **Botanical Gardens**. While we're in Gojo we shop the artisan handcrafts at **Mustard** and head to **Kitone Kyoto** in hopes of nabbing one of their exquisite limited-edition desserts. From there, we wind our way down to the beautiful **Kawai Kanjiro Memorial Museum** to see how the great mid-century ceramicist lived and worked.

Michelle explores the range of immaculate stationery at **Uragu**, sorts through linen at **Nomura Tailor**, peruses the beautiful creations at **Minä Perhonen** or pops over to **Box&Needle** to do a craft workshop. I hunt through vintage vinyl at **Joe's Garage** or **Happy Jacks** before hitting **efish** for a sly beer. It wouldn't be a perfect day without stopping by **Ippodo** for a whisked green tea and sweets. Together, we'll head north and float into **Stardust** for a raw cheesecake and organic wine before a soak at long-standing hot spring **Funaoka Onsen**. Then we'll pop in to **Sarasa Nishijin** for dinner, or we might stroll along the **Philosopher's Path** as dusk settles, heading to **Nanzen-ji**, where the low light creates a magical atmosphere over the tranquil Zen temple. This is also a good time to visit **Fushimi Inari** for a walk through the tunnel of tori gates before heading to **Kyo Apollo** for an izakaya (gastropub) feast. For dessert, we head to **Cafe TaBCo** for a deliciously sweet taiyaki (fish-shaped cake), paired with great music and a Heartland beer. We often find ourselves at the wonderful **Cafe Independants** to round off this perfect day.

# KYOTO OVERVIEW

Kita-ku

11

Ukyo-ku

8

京都市
KYOTO-SHI

Kamigyo-ku

7

10

9

4

Nakagyo-ku

3

6

Kameoka-shi

2

5

Shimogyo-ku

1

Higashiyama-ku

京都府
KYOTO-FU

Minami-ku

Nishikyo-ku

Muko-shi

Fushimi-ku

Nagaokakyo-shi

大阪府
OSAKA-FU

Kumiyamacho

12

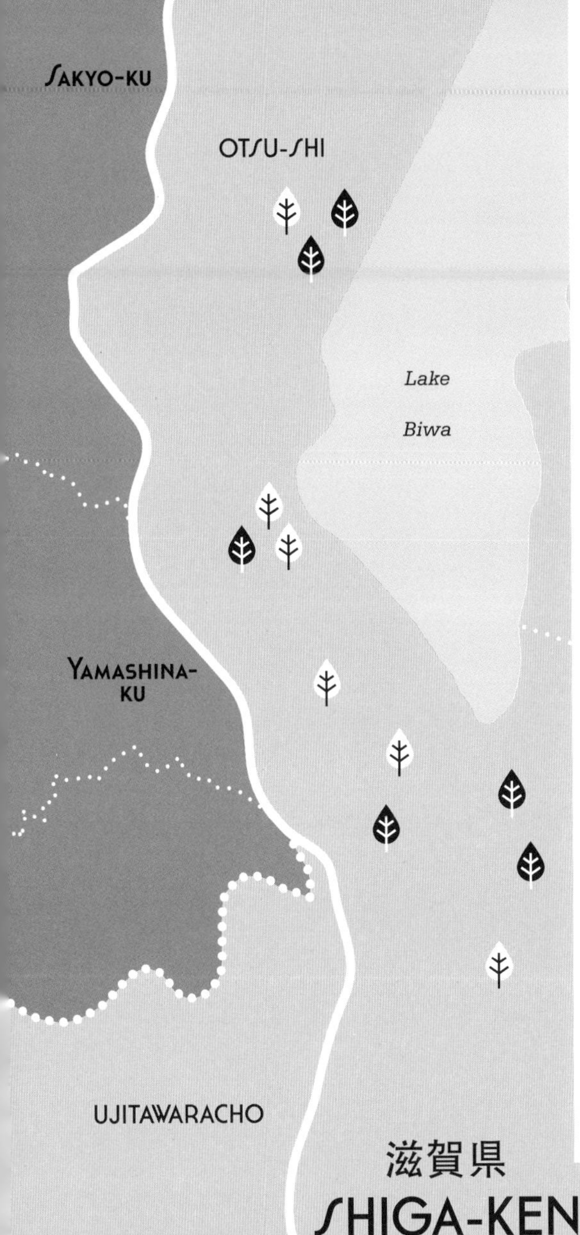


## PRECINCTS

1. Kyoto Station
2. Gojo
3. Shijo
4. Sanjo and Teramachi
5. South Higashiyama
6. Gion
7. North Higashiyama
8. North Kyoto
9. Nijo

## FIELD TRIPS

10. Arashiyama
11. The Eizan Line
12. The Nara Line

### KYOTO ADDRESS SYSTEM

A Japanese address is confusing, but a Kyoto address is something else! Translated, you may end up with something like 'through the Yaki underpass and left at Mrs Tanaka's house'. It's charming, but confounding. This key to Kyoto's addresses is here to help.

府 -fu = prefecture
市 -shi = city
区 -ku = ward
町 cho = town, or sub-region of a ward
通 dori = street
北 kita = north
南 minami = south
東 higashi = east
西 nishi = west
agaru = north of, or above
sagaru = south of, or below

# KYOTO STATION

Kyoto's sparse southern zone is most notable for Kyoto Station, a monolithic structure that competes with Kyoto's ancient temples and shrines for 'landmark' status, and does an admirable job. Chances are you'll be using this as a jumping-off point to explore Kyoto's tourist hot spots, and the area around the station won't be number one on your to-do list. But it's not just a pick-up and drop-off point – the station can amuse you for hours with a wide range of shopping and eating opportunities including department stores, malls and even a ramen village.

Your first impression south of Kyoto Station will be gaudy pachinko (pinball) parlours, faceless malls and electronics superstores, but if you zoom in you'll find an up-and-coming suburb with new cafes, inventive hotels and vibrant local and multicultural eateries – all overseen by the towering five-storied pagoda of the wonderful Toji Temple. North of the station you'll find the Kyoto Tower – a bright monolith with an observation deck that commands spectacular views of Kyoto.

SIGHTS
1. Kyoto Station
2. Kyoto Tower
3. Toji Temple
SHOPPING
4. Hirata Kyodo Gangu-ten
SHOPPING AND EATING
5. Toji flea market
6. Kyoto Station shopping
7. Isetan
EATING AND DRINKING
8. Kyoto Station ramen koji
9. Lower East 9 Hostel

## 1. KYOTO STATION

[MAP 2 D2]

Emerging from the platform into the station's main hall is a real 'wow' moment. Kyoto Station is often ranked as one of the top five things to see in a city boasting the most stunning shrines and temples in the world. The towering ceiling, vast arrivals and departures hall and an escalator that disappears into the heavens are benchmarks of contemporary design and construction. With hotels, eateries and shopping malls, the station is almost its own suburb. Head to the skywalk, 45 metres (147 feet) above the central gate, to get a sense of the city and its surrounding mountains.

## 2. KYOTO TOWER

[MAP 2 D2]

At 131 metres (430 feet) tall, this space-age monolith is your first photo op outside Kyoto Station. Built in 1964, locals were no fans of the modern structure, which was costly to construct and out of keeping with the city's timeless beauty. But this mid-century ugly duckling is now in vogue. The tower has shops, a hotel and an observation tower (¥770 will get you into the Jetsons-style viewing platform for wide-angle views of the city). Head down to the basement for a leisurely soak at **YUU** bathhouse, then head up to **KUU** for cocktails with a view.

**KYOTO STATION**
901 Karasuma dori,
Higashishiokojicho,
Shimogyo-ku
Mon–Sun 8.30am–7pm

**KYOTO TOWER**
721-1 Karasuma dori,
Higashishiokojicho,
Shimogyo-ku
Mon–Sun 9am–9pm

**POCKET TIP**
Visit Bic Camera or Yodobashi for all your electronic needs.

## 3. TOJI TEMPLE

[MAP 2 A4]

Toji Temple, or 'East' Temple, stands on one side of the Rashomon gate, the entrance to Japan's original capital. The 'west' temple, Saiji, is no longer with us – it burnt down in 1233 and was not rebuilt – but Toji remains, a testament to the striking temples that would once have greeted you as you rode into the city with your cart full of silks and spices. Dating back to 796, the Buddhist temple's treasures include a five-storey pagoda – the tallest wooden tower in Japan – the **Kondo** (golden hall), with its ancient statue of Yakushi the medicine Buddha, and the **Miedo Hall**. A stroll in the gardens during cherry blossom season in the spring is a magical experience. The ¥800 entry fee includes entrance to the pagoda's ground level, allowing you to delve deeper into the wonders of a structure that's over 1200 years old. For treasure hunters, there's a hugely popular flea market held in the grounds on the 21st of each month (*see* p. 5).

**TOJI TEMPLE**
1 Kujo dori, Kujocho, Minami-ku
Toji Station or bus no 19, 202, 207, 208
Mon–Sun 8.30am–5.30pm

## 4. HIRATA KYODO GANGU-TEN

89 Tojihigashimonzencho,
Minami-ku
681 5896
http://tab.do/items/18249492
Mon–Sun 9am–5pm
[MAP 2 B3]

Turn left as you leave the east gate of **Toji Temple** (*see* p. 3), spin around three times, say the magic words and you'll see a small row of old, mysterious shops. In the middle of these shops you'll find a small, vintage store with a small, vintage owner. Ninety-six-year-old Hirata opened this jumbled curiosity shop in 1976, herding pre-loved oddities onto shelves, cramming them into glass cabinets and stacking them in teetering piles. Here you'll find everything from retro maneki-neko (lucky cats) to buddha statuettes, noh masks and kokeshi dolls (pictured at right). Prices vary from 'bargain' to 'this piece must be very rare'. Sidle your way carefully around the haphazard collection and you're bound to find something enchanting (or possibly enchanted) to take home with you.

**POCKET TIP**
Check out cool indie cinema Minami Kaikan.

## 5. TOJI FLEA MARKET

1 Kujo dori, Kujocho,
Minami-ku
691 3325
toji.or.jp
21st of each month, 9am–4.30pm
[MAP 2 A4]

Once a month, under the benevolent gaze of the five-tiered pagoda, a festive, bustling flea market bursts into life in the usually peaceful grounds of **Toji Temple** (*see* p. 3). Go at lunchtime and try some of Kyoto's best street food. Tentacle on a stick, anyone? Be brave. Point and smile, even if you don't know what you're ordering – chances are you'll be going back for more. Join locals and tourists raiding brightly bannered stalls for vintage kimonos, '60s and '70s toys, lacquerware, fabrics, kewpie dolls, pottery, fans, swords, tea kettles and wood block prints. A smaller and less crowded antique market is held at Toji Temple on the first Sunday of each month.

## 6. KYOTO STATION SHOPPING

901 Karasuma dori,
Higashishiokojicho,
Shimogyo-ku
361 4401
www.kyoto-station-building.co.jp/English
Shop hours vary
[MAP 2 D2]

Kyoto Station teems with travellers arriving and departing in a flurry of activity. There's still time to eat and shop though. Within the station's arrival and departure gates you'll find stores selling colourful, seasonal bento (takeout) boxes packed with delicious gems. Your senses will be overloaded by packs of pickles, shelves of sake, sweets, souvenirs and more. Once out of the gate you'll find pitstop versions of the city's pickle, sweets and rice cracker specialists – check out **Kyo Miyagi** for a colourful range of irresistible treats. Head to **Kyoto-Saryo** for superb-quality green tea and wagashi (traditional Japanese sweets). The station has two 'shopping malls', called **The Cube** and **Porta**, with quintessential Japan-style shopping. Try a Kyoto pour-over coffee at **Ogawa**, or snack on takoyaki balls at **Gindaico**. Junk-food or coffee addicts can pick up a brew and the super cute Pon De Lion at **Mr Donut**.

**POCKET TIP**
Visit blockbuster Muji and Uniqlo stores at the Aeon Mall.

## 7. ISETAN

JR Isetan Kyoto
901 Karasuma dori,
Higashishiokojicho,
Shimogyo-ku
352 1111
http://kyoto.wjr-isetan.co.jp
Mon–Sun 10am–8pm
[MAP 2 D2]

Isetan is one of Japan's most sophisticated department stores, and the Kyoto Station branch is no exception. With everything from fashion to homewares, you could nab a bargain or spend up big on a designer label – either way, the shopping is excellent. But it's the food hall that you'll really flip over: two floors crammed with Kyoto delicacies that put paid to the idea that department stores can't do quality eating. You'll spend hours wandering around, ogling the chicken and beef bento (takeout) boxes, coveting perfectly shaped sushi, going crackers for crackers in a range of mind-boggling flavours and getting sweet on desserts that burst with colour. You're sure to buy more than you can eat, but that's half the fun. The jewelled boxes of biscuits or candies make for perfect gifts – if they make it to your friends, that is! Craft beer enthusiasts will be blown away by the selection.

## 8. KYOTO STATION RAMEN KOJI

10F, JR Isetan Kyoto
Karasuma dori, Shiokoji Sagaru,
Shimogyo-ku
365 2077
kyoto-ramen-koji.com
Mon–Sun 11am–10pm
[MAP 2 D2]

It's a long journey into the clouds on a slow escalator, but there's something a bit 'Jack and the Beanstalk' about this mystical land of ramen. Kyoto Station's ramen alley offers ramen makers from eight different prefectures. Tuck into the no-nonsense Workers' Delight or the flavour-packed Osakan Araumado, or discover the deep, multi-layered mysteries of the Tokyo Taishoken. Broths aren't just pork – **Menya Iroha** does a fish-based soy sauce broth, although vegaquarians should note that it may still arrive with pork slices. Try their famously addictive Toyama Black. Buy a ticket at the vending machine at the front – many have an English button. Wash your ramen down with a beer and make liberal use of the pickles. It's cheap and fun, and there are plenty of pictures, and even some English descriptions, to guide you through your ramen adventure.

**POCKET TIP**
Don't feel like ramen? Head to Kobe's famous Gavly Burger on the same floor.

## 9. LOWER EAST 9 HOSTEL

32 Kujo dori, Higashikujo
Minamikarasumacho,
Minami-ku
644 9990
http://lowereastnine.com
Mon–Sun 8am–11pm
[MAP 2 D4]

Small and shinily new, open from sunrise to sunset, Lower East 9 Hostel is the poster hostel and cafe for the reinvention of Kyoto Station South. Dwelling happily on the corner of a vast intersection a stone's throw from **Kujo Station**, this ultra-cool New York–style hostel offers a sparse, minimalist space warmed up with vintage furniture, comfy couches and the welcoming smiles of the very friendly staff. Grab a window seat and sink into one of the cosy green velvet chairs, order a craft beer while reading the latest Kyoto lifestyle mag, or order a glass of wine and mingle with locals and international travellers. The cafe does great coffee in the morning – if you're finding a good brew a bit hard to come by, you won't be disappointed here. At night the happy hour is fuelled by well-priced booze and complemented by a soundtrack of the latest smooth grooves.

# GOJO

Tucked neatly between Kyoto Station and Shijo, Gojo can be overlooked in a city that has so much to offer. This is a great shame because there are many gems hidden on and around the main thoroughfare of Gojo dori. Beautiful examples of residential houses with artfully arranged bonsai gardens and bicycles out the front sit alongside pickle shops, boutique hotels and tiny standing bars. This understated area is where you'll find the latest designer or the perfect bento (takeout) box lunch. Gojo dori may appear to be good for driving along and little else, but if you dig a little deeper you'll find handcraft stores nestled in the depths of buildings, old eateries tucked between tower blocks on the street and new and established stores sitting side-by-side on alleys, lanes and streets that trickle off the main drag. The area around the Bukkoji Temple and Lantern Street is home to some of the most interesting examples of artisan and concept retail stores, around which a burgeoning cafe scene has emerged. Further east, the canals offer tranquil walks and unique shopping experiences. Just far enough from Shijo to be a secret and near enough to Kyoto Station to be relevant, Gojo has had a complete renaissance.

SIGHTS
1. Higashi Honganji
2. Bukkoji
SHOPPING
3. Mustard
SHOPPING AND EATING
4. Kitone Kyoto
5. D&Department
6. D&Department Shokudo
7. Jimukino Ueda building
8. efish
9. Kaikado
EATING AND DRINKING
10. Cafe Marble
11. Cafe TaBCo
12. Sobanomi Arashiyama
Yoshimura
13. Saryo Suisen

# 1. HIGASHI HONGANJI

[MAP 1 B7, 2 D1]

'Now Life Is Living You', proclaims a sign on the walled moat around this unmissable temple compound that serves as the headquarters for one of the most popular sects of Buddhism in Japan, Jodo-shin (or True Pure Land). Taking up a huge chunk of real estate on Karasuma-dori, Higashi Honganji ushers you in through extraordinary black pressed-metal gates. The major drawcard, the spectacular main hall, is the largest wooden structure in Kyoto. The secret gem, though, is the **Hiunkaku Pavilion**, a surviving structure from the beginning of the Edo period. Higashi Honganji is just part of the story. Just to the west is the splendid **Nishi Honganji**, whose main attractions are **Goeido Hall** and **Amidado Hall**. A block to the east you'll find **Shosei-en**, a small and peaceful 'pond stroll' garden created in 675. Also known as Kikoku-tei because of a particular type of orange that once grew here, Shosei-en is a good spot for some cherry blossom viewing without the crowds.

**HIGASHI HONGANJI**
Karasuma dori, Tokiwacho, Shimogyo-ku
Gojo Station or bus no 9, 82, 205, 207, 208
Mon–Sun 5.50am–5.30pm (Mar–Oct), Mon–Sun 6.20am–4.30pm (Nov–Feb)

**BUKKOJI**
397 Bukkoji, Shinkaicho, Shimogyo-ku
Shijo or Hankyo Karasuma stations, or bus no 101
Mon–Sun 9am–4pm

**POCKET TIP**

Grab a coffee or lunch at Tsubomi, tucked behind the massive temple grounds.

## 2. BUKKOJI

[MAP 1 B5]

Bukkoji is also known as the 'Temple of the Buddha's Light'. Named after the ancient Bukkoji Buddhist sect, this temple officially opened in 1324, hitting its stride in the 1500s when it moved to the grounds where it resides today. Simple and unfussy, the religious building has a dark and interesting past featuring bandits, murders and untimely deaths. There is little evidence of this subversive plotline today, however. You can stroll in off the street – admission is free – and take your time walking around and enjoying the peaceful square. There is a small well with a presiding dragon, one of Kyoto's enduring images, as well as a shoro (bell tower). Followers of the Bukkoji sect have traditionally been lower-class peasants and artisan communities, so it's no surprise design store **D&Department** (*see* p. 16) chose to set up shop here, marking an interesting new chapter in the temple's story.

## 3. MUSTARD

588 Higashinotoin dori,
Torocho,
Shimogyo-ku
344 2455
mustard-3rd.com
Fri–Tues 11am–6pm
[MAP 1 B5]

As you enter this quiet corridor of retail beauty you'll feel the outside world fall away. Small, artfully arranged displays of seed pods, plants and paintings provide a backdrop for the handwoven knits that hang from the ceiling like pieces of art. The works of local jewellers and accessory designers perch on painted tree branches, bags and shoes sprout from plants, everything is connected to nature. Mustard makes original, handcrafted, handwoven products. The shawls, scarves and ultra-woolly jumpers here are pure quality, and the very definition of eco-friendly. Knits are handwoven on an original loom in Mustard's top-floor studio. Ask to see the upstairs gallery, a small, leaf-strewn space suffused with light that shows off their works in changing exhibitions. At ¥14,000–¥24,000 for scarves and shawls, and more for jumpers and throws, prices are an investment in local quality. In a world of mass production, the skill level here is something to be cherished.

# 4. KITONE KYOTO

1F, 589 Torocho,
Shimogyo-ku
352 2428
http://kitone.jp
Fri–Tues 12pm–nightfall
[MAP 1 B5]

In a tranquil pocket of calm near the **Byodoji Shrine**, a hinged garage door lifts up to reveal this rustic and beautiful store that doubles as a small cafe. The cult of Kitone reaches way beyond Kyoto. Tokyoites in the know make a beeline for the store, if not for limited-edition desserts that resemble small artworks then for their small but artfully collected cache of vintage and new ceramics, homewares, handmade accessories and oddments. Kitone have a keen eye for the best in simple quality. The tiny cafe has a communal table and a two-seater bench in a miniature backroom library. Try their shaved ice – they get adventurous with flavours like white kidney bean and wolfberry fruit alongside tried-and-true favourites such as apricot jam.

## 5. D&DEPARTMENT

397 Shinkaicho,
Shimogyo-ku
343 3217
www.d-department.com/jp/shop/kyoto
Mon–Fri 11am–6pm,
Sat–Sun 11am–8pm
[MAP 1 B5]

Here's your chance to worship at the shrine of design. This showcase for D&Department's perfectly curated selection is housed in a beautiful old building on the grounds of a Zen temple. A collaboration with the Kyoto School of Art and Design and the Shin-Buddhism Bukkoji Temple faction, D&Department's contemporary aesthetic sits perfectly within these ancient surroundings. Meditate upon the simple beauty of the objects – a mix of stationery, homewares, food products and more; the best of regional Japan brought together under one ancient roof. Many of these products are unique to Kyoto, such as utensils and knives made by local artisans. Don't miss the design gallery's changing exhibitions showing the latest works from the students at the design school. New design shaking hands with ancient beauty on the grounds of a tranquil temple that dates back to 1324 – only in Kyoto!

# 6. D&DEPARTMENT SHOKUDO

397 Shinkaicho,
Shimogyo-ku
343 3215
www.d-department.com/jp/shop/kyoto
Mon–Sun 11am–6pm,
closed Wed
[MAP 1 C5]

If you want to see what modernism looked like in Japan in the '60s, and enjoy the privilege of eating lunch while gazing at a Zen temple, make this your food destination. As soon as you slip off your shoes and walk across the tatami (straw) mats you know you're in for a special experience. This beautiful old building is where the monks used to make and prepare tea. Now it's the spiritual home of a lunch set that comes in at around ¥1100, showcasing light seasonal vegetable dishes with rice and soup. Soak up the atmosphere while ordering a specialty roasted coffee with a dessert of green tea ice-cream and red beans. In warmer months the sliding doors of the cafeteria are opened, giving you a beautiful view of the temple.

## 7. JIMUKINO UEDA BUILDING

21 Takakura dori, Sakaicho, Shimogyo-ku
341 4111
ueda-h.co.jp
Mon–Sun 11.30am–12am
[MAP 1 B6]

The sliding door of an unassuming office block on Gojo dori reveals the *Mad Men*-meets-retro office interior of the Jimukino Ueda building. In this stylish block, built in 1968, you can still hear the feet of sharply dressed office workers tapping up and down the stairs. **Box&Needle** run the show here – a crafter's paradise that is home to beautiful patterned papers that make their way onto all manner of journals, fans and, most prominently, boxes. Floor-to-ceiling shelves are crammed with a huge range of paper craft heaven. Enquire about their workshops where you can try your hand at box making and decorating. If you get hungry, grab an organic lunch set at **Punto Punto** on the ground floor, a cool canteen that specialises in fresh local produce with a preference for vegetables and rice. Don't miss the **Yamahon Homewares Gallery**, a small space that exhibits one-off artisan arts and crafts, including paintings, prints, handmade ceramics and lacquerware.

**POCKET TIP**

Classic paper store Morita Washi has beautiful artisan paper.

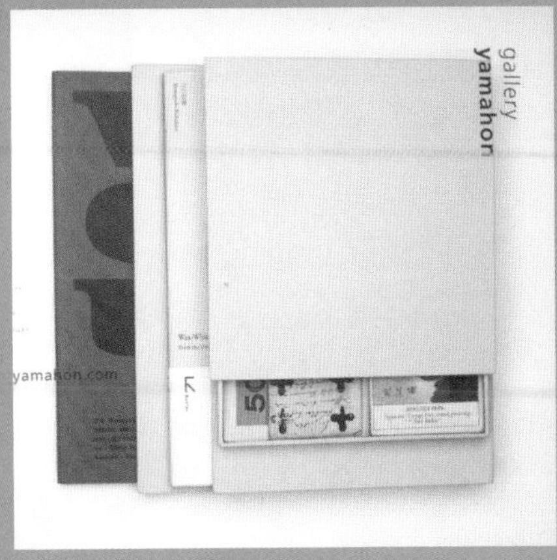

gallery
yamahon
yamahon.com

ORIGINAL
puntopunto
size: 945 × 635mm

## 8. EFI/H

798–1 Kiya-machi dori,
Nishihashizumecho,
Shimogyo-ku
361 3069
shinproducts.com/efish
Mon–Sun 10am–10pm
[MAP 1 C6]

Follow the black cat to catch the efish – a laid-back, in-the-know Kyoto hangout where you can kick back and sip booze at any time of day. Window seats are so close to the river you're almost swimming in it. In the summer months the wide windows are thrown open, making this the perfect spot to sit back and take in some nature. The decor is mid-century modern meets industrial warehouse, with vintage furniture, hanging lights and pre-loved antiques. A young clientele enjoys the Western-influenced menu with plenty of vegetarian options. Drinks are plentiful, with an extensive juice menu and a booze selection that leans towards the retro end of the scale (tequila sunrise, anyone?). Items by former Apple designer Shin Nishibori (efish was once his house) are still sold on site.

**POCKET TIP**

Sauna no Ume-yu is a cool Meiji-era onsen (hot spring) run by a 24-year-old and aimed at a younger clientele.

# 9. KAIKADO

84–1 Umeminatocho,
Shimogyo-ku
351 5788
kaikado.jp
Mon–Sun 12pm–6pm
[MAP 1 C7]

Kaikado are famous for their perfectly turned and expertly crafted tin plate chazutsu (Japanese tea canisters). This family of master craftsmen have kept their dream alive through six generations, with each successor bringing a unique edge to the business. Their clean, simple and timeless approach has been applied to their latest venture: this stylish new cafe. The exterior is industrial chic, exposed brick with large sliding windows of steel and glass, while the tea canister designs are echoed in the hanging lamps and the stark, minimalist lines of the interior. The beautiful chazutsu are on display in big blonde wooden cabinets, and can be bought here. Or you can just stop by for the wide range of top-quality tea and coffee, and cheesecake shaped just like the tea canisters.

# 10. CAFE MARBLE

378 Bukkoji dori, Nishimaecho, Shimogyo-ku
634 6033
cafe-marble.com
Mon–Sat 11.30am–10pm, Sun 11.30am–8pm
[MAP 1 C5]

Park your hired bike out the front and join the Kyoto locals at Cafe Marble. What was once an old machiya (traditional wooden townhouse) is now an impressively beautiful and cosy space, the stomping ground for locals, artists and friends having afternoon tea. Inside you'll find museum-like old-world charm, with ancient bureaus and cabinets, worn wooden bookshelves and mid-century ceramics softened by big comfy couches, flower arrangements and graphics of a cutesy bear and bird. The youthful staff will greet you with a cheery 'irrashaimase' (welcome) and serve you French/Italian-themed food like freshly baked seasonal tarts and quiches. Be sure to try the intriguingly named Jam Soda. Take a seat on the long table – it's the perfect place to do a spot of work. On the way out you can grab the cafe's own products, tenugui (hand towels) and postcards, all designed on the premises.

## 11. CAFE TABCO

463 Senshojicho,
Shimogyo-ku
755 6282
http://cafetabco.com
Thurs–Tues 11.30–12am
[MAP 1 C5]

You can tell this place is owned by a music lover – the interior is filled with guitars (I counted six), amps and a piano, and the walls are covered with posters promoting upcoming events. This cosy downstairs lair with music, good food and easy drinking is a great night-time hangout, judging by the polaroids of good times plastered on the wall. Beer, whiskey and wine come in at around ¥500–¥600. Have a few too many and you may find yourself joining in on one of the open mic sessions. The basement's vibe is ramshackle op-shop chic, complete with musical note clock, crystal flowers and fairy lights. Food is simple and tasty – think curry and pasta washed down with Heartland beer. Definitely order some honey butter naan, but don't fill up. People flock here for the taiyaki (pictured at left) – a crispy, fish-shaped pastry filled with delicious red bean paste and served up with ice cream and delectable grilled banana that's candied in the skin.

## 12. SOBANOMI YOSHIMURA

420 Gojo dori, Matsuyacho,
Shimogyo-ku
353 0114
arashiyama-yoshimura.com/soba/sobanomi
Mon–Sun 11am–2.30pm
5.30–10.30pm
[MAP 1 B6]

Nestled among the faceless facades on the broad swathe of Gojo dori you'll find this surprising piece of old Kyoto. Sobanomi Yoshimura belies its location and delivers one of Kyoto's most atmospheric, inexpensive soba experiences. Not only will the price make you smile, but the soba is made fresh on the premises – you can watch the soba masters in action, working that dough into beautiful, perfectly chewy noodles. Other dishes range from chicken wings to tempura and sashimi, which are all equally impressive. Why not have a sake or two, delivered in small squares of luminous glassware? Sip it while watching the world go by from the upstairs window, or slide into a booth downstairs for some real Kyoto 'fast food'.

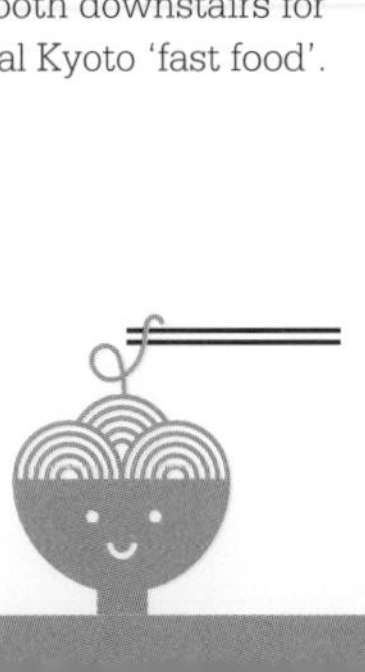

## 13. SARYO SUISEN

521 Takatsuji dori, Inaricho,
Shimogyo-ku
278 0111
http://saryo-suisen.com
Thurs–Tues 10am–6pm
[MAP 1 B5]

Saryo Suisen is regarded as one of the go-to places for a Kyoto-style sugar hit. This famous old-school tea cafe does all the classics, but impeccably well. You could order a green tea with a tiny, precious wagashi (sweet) for ¥680, but this is no time to be a Puritan – you've come here for an over-the-top dessert. The roll cake is a good choice at ¥480, but the coup de grâce is the towering matcha parfait (pictured at left). This '50s sundae-style dessert with sponge, matcha ice-cream, red beans, glutinous rice balls, chiffon cake and dusted jelly is well worth the ¥1390 it will set you back. This is the queen of Kyoto desserts, and it's perfect for sharing. You'll see friends on a day out, lunching ladies and grown men who should know better, doing just that.

# SHIJO

If you thought Kyoto was all about temples and gardens, think again. Home to world-class shopping and eating, this mini city with a country atmosphere has the best of the best. Shijo dori is a busy shopping street, cutting a majestic swathe through the heart of Kyoto, but it has somehow managed to absorb the Zen-like calm of the mountains and temples that overlook it. Locals and visitors flock here to shop at name department stores, chic boutiques and every other retail experience you can imagine. If it's souvenirs you're after, you won't be disappointed.

Get your bearings here, as it's the perfect jumping-off point for most of your Kyoto to-do list. The river is to the east, Nijo Castle and the splendid bamboo groves of Arashiyama are to the west, and all around you is a panoramic view of the beautiful mountains. For a reprieve from shopping, head to the back streets for small makers, tiny cafes, old-school noodle joints and the Nishiki Market, Kyoto's unmissable foodie experience. Take a stroll through old Kyoto's atmospheric night-life district Pontocho, the peaceful grounds at Rokkaku-do or the picturesque back streets around the canals.

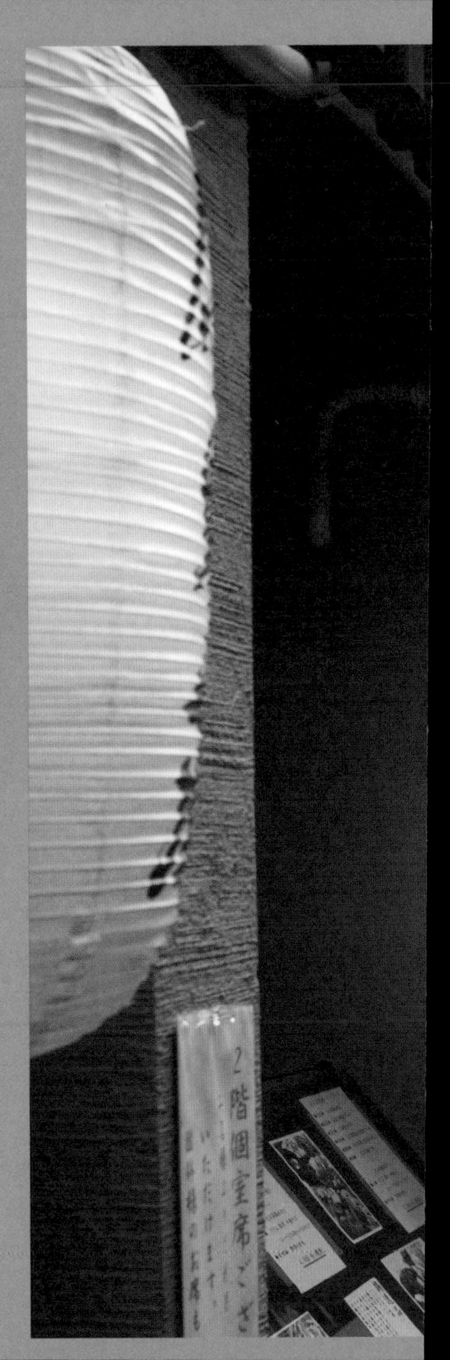

SIGHTS
1. Pontocho
2. Rokkaku-do
SHOPPING
3. Joe's Garage
4. Sou Sou
5. Shijo shopping
6. Nomura Tailor
7. Minä Perhonen
8. Lisn
SHOPPING, EATING AND DRINKING
9. Nishiki Market
10. Rokkaku dori
EATING AND DRINKING
11. Kiln
12. AWOMB
13. Gogyo
14. Kyo Apollo
15. Soirée
16. Yuka riverside dining
伏見の清酒
伏見蔵

# 1. PONTOCHO

[MAP 1 D4]

This is Edo's pleasure zone – a narrow street crammed with tiny bars, eateries and beautifully preserved townhouses where geisha and maiko (apprentice geisha) have tip-tapped between appointments in exclusive tea houses and clubs since the 1600s. Kabuki (highly stylised drama) actors, sumo wrestlers and more than a few shady characters come here to let off steam, and there's no reason why you shouldn't join them. Put it on your late-night drinking list – opening hours run from dusk to midnight. Cobblestones, lanterns and small illuminated signs will draw you into the street's timeless magic. Good bars to drink in include **FSN Chez Philippe** and **Hello Dolly**. But be brave; adventure awaits down alleys and up stairs, and after a drink or two you might find yourself channelling your inner samurai or wannabe geisha. Seedy bars, eye-bogglingly expensive bills, the gaudy, the crass and the beautiful – you'll find it all here in this slice of old Kyoto.

## 2. ROKKAKU-DO

[MAP 1 B3]

Resisting the looming presence of surrounding office towers, this Heian-period Buddhist temple remains a peaceful haven where you can enjoy tranquility and, in the right season, willow trees and cherry blossoms. Tiny, cheeky Buddha statues are artfully placed on rocks and in and about flower arrangements and twisted trees. Check out the one inside the main hall in a gentle state of trance – or perhaps he's just fallen asleep. What makes Rokkaku-do really special is that it's the birthplace of ikebana (flower arranging). The priest Sankei Ikenobo, who had a talent for arranging flowers, created a new way to present them as an offering to Kannon, the goddess of mercy. The tradition was continued, and an iconic Japanese craft was born. You'll find the Ikenobo school right next door – pop inside to read up on the history of ikebana and sign up for a traditional ikebana course.

**PONTOCHO**
Pontocho dori, Matsumotocho, Nakagyo-ku
Shijo Station, Kawaramachi Station, or bus no 17, 205

**ROKKAKU-DO**
248 Rokkaku dori, Donomaecho, Nakagyo-ku
Karasuma Oike Station or bus no 9, 101
Mon–Sun 6am–5pm

## 3. JOE'S GARAGE

2F Tomishaya Bldg
572 Takakura dori, Obiyacho, Nakagyo-ku
241 0277
jgarage.com
Mon–Sun 12–10pm
[MAP 1 C4]

Only in Japan would you find a store that takes its name from a Frank Zappa LP and uses Andy Warhol's iconic banana as its logo, but somehow it sums up the eclectic mix of music on offer in this small but perfectly pitched record store. There are many small record shops in Kyoto and each has its own specialty. Joe's Garage is all about soul, jazz and rock, with a smattering of vintage western rock and Japanese experimental discs. But before the thrill of the vinyl hunt begins, you'll have to get out your map and compass to find the store. Climb the stairs and enter through a small craft and pom pom shop. Once you're inside, assume the position: head down with fingers flicking through record after record until you pluck out that long sought-after classic.

## 4. SOU SOU

583–3 Nakanocho,
Nakagyo-ku
212 8805
sousou.co.jp
Mon–Sun 11am–8pm
[MAP 1 D4]

Renowned Kyoto textile design house Sou Sou create their own vibrant and colourful patterns to adorn the old (kimonos and monks' working clothes) and the new (smart phone covers, purses, notebooks and more). People flock to the store to grab 'tabi' (split toe) socks that come in a range of vivid patterns. Footwear here is also an eye-opener. Check out the geta (Japanese sandals), a hybrid toe shoe crossed with trainers crossed with gumboots and complete with Sou Sou's vibrant colours and designs. The main storefront is instantly recognisable: a yellow square covered in black numbers, the famous Sou Sou logo that you can find on many of their products. This area just off the main streets has been dubbed Sou Sou Street by the locals – you'll find seven diverse stores in this cute little enclave.

## 5. SHIJO SHOPPING

[MAP 1 B E4]

Shijo dori has a permanently festive atmosphere, with canopies, piped music, hanging banners and seasonal displays. This is the perfect place to start the day if you need a Kyoto shopping fix. Head to DIY superstore **Tokyu Hands** for a prime pick of their famous selection of homewares, gadgets and gizmos. Stationery nerds, rejoice: this store is your holy grail. Check out **Daimaru** and **Takashimaya** for top-level department store shopping, and don't miss their basement food halls crammed with delicious food with a Kyoto twist. Daimaru's hip little sister, **Fuji Daimaru**, stocks contemporary fashion for the younger set. Sweets fans should drop by **O Tabi Kyoto** for some quality matcha soft serve or wonderfully packaged Kyoto specialties, which are perfect for gifts. When your feet are sore and you need a Kyoto-style pick-me-up, try **Toraya**'s precious green tea wagashi (sweet) gems. Heading towards Gion, you'll find some smaller zakka (everyday items) stores. **Handkerchief Bakery** has lovely handkerchiefs, and **Karancolon Kyoto** and **RAAK** have great fabric bags and scarves made with Kyoto-designed textiles.

## 6. NOMURA TAILOR

362 Shijo dori, Naramonocho,
Shimogyo-ku
212 4679
nomura-tailor.co.jp
Mon–Sun 10am–7.30pm
[MAP 1 C4]

This world-class fabric mecca is a one-stop shop for the crafty crafter, sewing enthusiast and Japanese-textile obsessive. If you need it, they have it. Linens, cottons and weaves are all superb quality and come in incredibly beautiful patterns, both traditional and modern. Rolls of fabric are piled high or found leaning against walls – riffle through them to find the latest designs or a classic kimono print. Accessories take up two of the three floors – cotton, needle and thread, wool, buttons, beads and, yes, even baubles come in all manner of shapes and sizes. There should be something here to enhance even the most well-stocked craft cave. Kyoto is known for handcrafts, and Nomura Tailor display their own examples on inspiration walls to help get your creative juices flowing. So why not buy up and make your own little something?

**POCKET TIP**
If you show your passport at Kyoto Tokyu Hands, you get a five per cent discount.

## 7. MINÄ PERHONEN

251–2 Karawamachi dori,
Ichinocho,
Shimogyo-ku
353 8990
mina-perhonen.jp/
Mon–Sun 12–8pm
[MAP 1 D5]

Worth a trip for the iconic building alone, the Kyoto branch of Minä Perhonen is a must for fans of designer Akira Minagawa's beautiful creations. The stunning Showa-era building from the 1920s–30s is devoted almost entirely to Minä. The first floor is the main store, and it's beautiful – the ceiling, tiled floor and butterfly-themed doors are worth a look, even if you aren't in the market for Minä's wistful and strikingly patterned designs. Climb to the third floor for Arkistot's jewellery and homewares selection; drool at the range in the galleria, cruelly showing clothing from earlier collections not available for sale. The fourth floor features Minä Piece (peer through the hole in the wall to see them hard at work sewing and repairing). The fabric bags and cloth-covered buttons are definite standouts.

**POCKET TIP**

Don't miss Merry Go Round bookshop on the Minä building's top floor, and a gallery showcasing local illustrators.

## 8. LISN

COCON Karasuma
620 Suiginyacho,
Shimogyo-ku
353 6466
lisn.co.jp
Mon–Sun 11am–8pm
[MAP 1 B4]

Relax and let the heavenly scents at Lisn speak to you. Lisn is the contemporary face of Kyoto's famous 300-year-old 'Shoyeido' incense store, and their timeless beauty has been brought up to date with exquisite contemporary packaging and delicate new spins on traditional aromas. The store is extraordinary. Walls curve like smoke, alien lights diffuse an otherworldy glow and shelves hang in the air like a waft of incense. A choice buyers' pick is the boxed selection of Lisn's most popular and engaging scents. It's the perfect souvenir, and a great way to bring the intoxicating aromas of Kyoto home with you.

# 9. NISHIKI MARKET

Nishikikoji dori,
Nakagyo-ku
kyoto-nishiki.or.jp
Tues–Sun 9am–5pm
[MAP 1 C4]

This thin alleyway crammed with stalls, eateries and street vendors isn't called the 'kitchen of Kyoto' for nothing. It's all about Japanese cuisine here, with a focus on Kyoto specialties. That means strange seafood grilled on sticks, a range of tea, sweets, crackers, soft-serve ice-cream (in matcha and black sesame flavours, among others) and colourful barrels brimming with all things pickled and fermented. Grab a burdock root or sweet potato stick and wash it down with a yuzu (a type of citrus fruit) juice. Vintage booze posters hold ramshackle izakayas (gastropubs) together. Slide in, perch on an upturned milk crate and order up a storm. Join the queue at **Sawawa** for some matcha warabi-mochi (powdered sweet jelly). The variety is staggering, but take a chance – you're sure to get an education. Nishiki Market is also a great place to buy Japanese knives. Head to **Aritsugu** for a selection that draws chefs and cooks from all corners of the world. There'll be an endless sea of people, but that's what a market is meant to be – bustling, loud and crazy.

一番搾り
うどん
グリーンティ
GREEN TEA
220円
ゆずジュース
YUZU JUICE
220円
アップルマンゴージュース
220円
牛すじ大根
220円

京の青菜
みぶ菜漬
1324

イカ

生クリーム
ビスコ
クリームサンドビスケット
6袋入
2枚×12パック
glico
おいしくてつよくなる
Cream
Collon
62円引き!!
お買得品!!

1本
¥450
¥450
¥450
¥450

# 10. ROKKAKU DORI

109 Rokkaku dori, Horinouecho, Nakagyo-ku
[MAP 1 C3]

For a break from bustling Shijo dori, head to Rokkaku dori for small maker stores, family-run businesses and long-standing eateries. **Rokkaku**'s range of letterpress papers, cards and envelopes is stunning. Enter **Suuzando Hashimoto** through the noren (traditional fabric) curtains and you'll find a colourful range to suit all your papercraft needs. And don't miss the oldest sweet shop in Japan, **Daigokuden Honpo**, established in 1885 and specialising in kohaku nagashi, a jelly made from seaweed starch that's dunked in homemade syrup. Look for the Japanese fan on the side of **Miyawaki Baisen-an**. They've been selling painted, scented fans here since 1823. A quick detour up Higashinotoin dori will bring you to **Yaoichi**, a premium supermarket with an array of products from around the world, plus fresh produce, a deli and plenty of booze. When you get hungry, head to **Kyo Apollo** (*see* p. 43), or chicken bar **Kazamidori** (look for the big chicken out the front!). Finish with a drink at ultra-cool **Bar K-ya**.

## 11. KILN

2F, Murakamijuu Bldg
194 Sendocho,
Shimogyo-ku
853 3555
http://kilnrestaurant.jp
Thurs–Tues 12–3pm, 6–11pm
[MAP 1 D4]

New-kid-on-the-block Kiln is a 20-seat cafe where you can lazily sip craft beer or housemade liqueur while overlooking a picturesque canal. The coffee here is single origin, and big blackboards in Kanji and English fill you in on the cake or sandwich of the day. Add an almond, chocolate or cassis biscotti to your order, or the delicious chocolate and kumquat scone, and groove along to smooth jazz. The view of the canal through floor-to-ceiling windows is perfect for gazing over cherry blossoms or autumn leaves. Come at night, too – the pizza joint upstairs kicks into gear as the sun goes down, and is a popular haunt for locals.

## 12. AWOMB

189 Takoyakushi dori,
Ubayanagicho,
Nakagyo-ku
204 5543
awomb.com
Mon–Sun 12–3pm, 6–9pm
[MAP 1 A3]

Word has spread about this sushi restaurant with a difference. They specialise in a kind of do-it-yourself sushi, self-termed teori–zushi (teori meaning 'origin' or 'foundation'), where you get all the base ingredients and roll your own. It's happy snap heaven – spectacular jewelled sashimi, spices, pickles, edible flowers and snow pea shoots are laid out on beautiful dark slate. Choose your flavour combination from the canvas of vibrant colours and textures. The novelty factor of being your own sushi chef makes this sophisticated fun. The room is stunning: superb architecture by Ujita Hiroshi reworks an old machiya (traditional wooden townhouse) into a minimalist warehouse space. You'll have to queue up (we waited for over two hours) at AWOMB – you can't book at lunchtime, and dinner is booked out a year in advance. You'll be served tea as you wait, and given a menu and a number to allay any fears that you might miss out on this special dining adventure.

## 13. GOGYO

452 Yanaginobanba dori,
Jumonjicho,
Nakagyo-ku
254 5567
ramendining-gogyo.com
Mon–Fri 11.30am–3pm,
6pm–12am, Sat 11.30am–4pm,
5pm–12am, Sun 11.30am–4pm,
5–11pm
[MAP 1 C4]

In a city with so many stories to tell, this building has one of the best. Before you even take your first slurp of the delicious ramen you'll be lost in the tale of former geisha Oyuki, who was wooed away from her lover and into marriage by JP Morgan's cashed-up nephew. When the nephew died, Oyuki returned to Japan, reconnected with her former beau and bought this beautiful machiya (traditional wooden town-houses) for them to live in. Head inside and take advantage of the house's transition into one of the most popular ramen joints in Japan. Inhale a bowl of smoky black, burnt miso ramen (pictured at bottom left) – it will easily make your top-five list. Sides of karage (fried chicken) or gyoza (dumplings) are cheap and delicious additions. Chances are you'll have to line up, but this is an experience that's worth waiting for.

# 14. KYO APOLLO

178 Rokkaku dori, Chigiriyacho, Nakagyo-ku
212 2233
kyo-apollo.jp
Mon–Sun 5pm–12am
[MAP 1 B3]

Rowdy locals pack this unpretentious izakaya (gastropub). They come for the atmosphere, but stay for the food, great beer and a tasting set of regional sake – three small cups of heaven! You can snack here or go to town for around ¥3500 per person, depending on your appetite. Ours was pretty big, so we had the fried camembert with raspberry sauce, their famous gyoza (dumplings), tasty yakitori (grilled meat), delicious fresh sashimi and some top-notch oden. The space is amazing but not imposing – an old Japanese house with wooden beams, cosy nooks and crannies, and a long table at the front if you're feeling communal (you will be after your sake tasting set). If you get a chance, sneak a peek at the beautiful banquet room at the back.

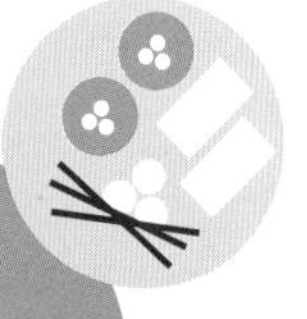

## 15. SOIRÉE

95 Shincho,
Shimogyo-ku
221 0351
aquadina.com/kyoto/spot/3817
Tues–Sun 1pm–7.30pm
[MAP 1 D4]

Emperor Showa reigned from the 1920s to the 1980s, and this cafe has a bit of every decade thrown in. It features two cosy floors of Swiss chalet chic, mock medieval ornate wood panelling, statuettes, hanging mirrors, ornate chandeliers and faux '70s light fixtures that glow over green vinyl benches. The result is one of the most oddball cafes you're ever likely to eat in. If you're a Kyoto-ite, chances are your grandparents came here on a date, and perhaps so have you. The clientele runs the whole gamut, from friends out for the afternoon to businessmen or lunching ladies pausing after a morning of serious shopping. It's gloriously chintzy, and although the menu is not in English, there are plenty of pictures of luminescent jelly drinks or over-the-top cakes and parfaits to point to.

# 16. YUKA RIVERSIDE DINING

Along the banks of the Kamo River

As spring gives way to summer and the intense heat starts to settle in for the season Kyoto feels the need to cool down – and so will you. What better way to do so than perched high above the river on yuka (platforms) built for the occasion, where you can eat and drink to the sound of gently flowing water. Over 90 different bars and restaurants here offer yuka. Each one has a different menu, so seek out the one that's right for you or go on a spree and try a few. Prices vary, but the experience doesn't need to be expensive. Get there before dusk (and the crowds) and sip sake while watching the lanterns come on along the river, illuminating the unfolding dark. Enjoy food, booze and stunning views of the eastern skyline while the breeze coming up from the Kamo River blows away the summer heat – it's the definition of romantic. No wonder it's been popular for over 400 years!

# SANJO AND TERAMACHI

As you head north from Shijo, Kyoto gets more tranquil, more refined, and a sense of history takes hold. Sanjo dori can feel more like a lazy stroll than a retail outing. Stores selling ceramics, lacquerware, kimonos and textiles will take you back to a time when craftsmanship and artisan stores still lined the strip. The artisan culture appears in both traditional and updated forms. Hunt for new lacquerware made the traditional way, or buy a kimono in contemporary colours and prints. Start your day in a long-established coffee shop or finish it off in a hip new bar. Teramachi dori runs perpendicular to Sanjo-dori and is known as the 'art avenue'. A stroll along this street takes in some of Kyoto's most renowned traditional craft stores. Fans of calligraphy, paper, antique textiles or tea simply should not miss it. Towards the north things start to get very peaceful – until you arrive at the Kyoto Imperial Palace, with its beautiful expanse of parklands. It's a great spot for picnicking or cycling, or to view cherry blossoms.

SIGHTS
1. Kyoto Imperial Palace
2. Nishiki Tenmangu Shrine
SHOPPING
3. Kyoto Design House
4. Kisshodo
5. Nijiyura
6. Wafukan Ichi
7. Gallery Kei
8. Kamiji Kakimoto
9. Happy Jack
10. Teramachi shopping
11. Ippodo
EATING AND DRINKING
12. Cafe Bibliotec Hello
13. Hitsuji
14. Inoda Coffee Honten
15. AB
16. Chisou Inaseya
17. Honke Owariya
18. Cafe Independants
19. Gyoza Chau

# 1. KYOTO IMPERIAL PALACE

[MAP 3 C5]

In the past, if you wanted to see the Imperial Palace you would have had to apply in advance at the Kunaicho, an office housed near the palace grounds or, for easier access, joined one of the infrequent tour groups. The good news is you can now enter and roam the grounds freely. The palace itself is quite modest, a low-roofed building with stark black-and-white shapes and simple lines. The emperors lived in the Imperial Palace from the 8th century until the end of the Edo period (1868). The surrounding **Kyoto Goyen** is a massive, sprawling park, a popular spot to view cherry blossoms and the colours of autumn. The northern part of the park is famous for ito-sakura, cherry blossoms that bloom early – so if you just can't wait, catch them here in late March and early April.

## 2. NISHIKI TENMANGU SHRINE

[MAP 1 C4]

In the heart of the covered arcade on Teramachi dori you'll find Nishiki Tenmangu. Modernity and consumerism mean the shrine is now hidden among retail spaces and pachinko (pinball) parlours. It's a popular spot with the many shoppers in the area and looks spectacular at night, when its lanterns are illuminated. The shrine is dedicated to the god of learning, and was set up as a place of worship for the workers and traders at the **Nishiki Market** (*see* p. 36–37). Though its well, which goes down to 300 metres (985 feet), may seem dark and mysterious, its water is apparently germ-free and okay to drink. The cow statue will bring you success in your studies, so go on and pat its head. You'll immediately feel smarter, and imbued with wisdom and a good head for business.

**KYOTO IMPERIAL PALACE**
3 Kyotogyoen, Kamigyo-ku
Imadegawa Station or bus no 102
Tues–Sun 9am–5pm

**NISHIKI TENMANGU SHRINE**
537 Nakanocho, Nakagyo-ku
Shijo Station or bus no 31, 46
Tues–Sun 8am–8pm

## 3. KYOTO DESIGN HOUSE

Tominokoji dori,
105 Fukunagacho,
Nakagyo-ku
221 0200
kyoto-dh.com/en
Mon–Sun 11am–8pm, closed last weekday of each month
[MAP 1 C3]

Even before you enter this chic design store, architect Tadao Ando sets the scene with his Niwaka building, a minimalist take on old-meets-new-meets-east-meets-west. Kyoto Design House is a fusion of traditional and modern Kyoto, and its modern artisans draw from the city's rich creative tradition. It may look imposing, but bringing beauty into the everyday is what Japan does best. There are many affordable items among the range of homewares, accessories and special pieces. Furoshiki (traditional wrapping cloth), shibori scarves, sake sets, jewellery and bags sit on shelves like gallery pieces. The blow-up washi paper fruit is beautiful and playful. The exquisite Sensuji loose-leaf tea caddies, minimal sake sets and super-cute robot charms made from used electronic parts are just a few of the 1500 items they have in store. Ask the charming English-speaking staff for the history of the pieces you're taking home.

## 4. KISSHODO

11 Sanjo dori, Nakanocho,
Nakagyo-ku
221 3955
kisshodo.jp
Tues–Sun 10am–7pm
[MAP 1 C3]

You could blink and almost miss this tiny, nondescript shopfront, but head inside and you'll think you've walked into a lacquerware museum. An eclectic, slightly ramshackle museum, perhaps – the collection can look a little bit thrown together – but make no mistake, the owner really knows his stuff. Kisshodo have been purveyors of lacquerware and crafts since 1924, and their shelves and cases show off some beautiful and delicate pieces. Thin, impossibly light soup and rice bowls, sake cups, wooden jewellery boxes and plates in shimmering red or black – you'll want to take them all home. You might pay a little more than at market stalls, but the quality and years of skill is reflected in these special objects.

## 5. NIJIYURA

38–1 Fuyacho dori,
Benkeiishicho,
Nakagyo-ku
253 0606
http://nijiyura.com
Mon–Sun 10am–8pm
[MAP 1 C3]

Tenugui are long, rectangular fabric pieces traditionally used for washcloths, dishcloths or even headbands (especially in martial art kendo, where they function as sweatbands). These days tenugui has become the perfect eco-wrapping for souvenirs, gifts or bottles of sake or beer. Nijiyura combines traditional dyeing and pattern-making techniques with contemporary materials, so you get the best of both worlds! This adorable little store just off Sanjo has a range of patterns, from colourful abstracted animals, birds and nature to more traditional Japanese emblems. In-store displays will show you how to manipulate your cloth into a carry bag, lunch box or wine holder. We like to take them home and use them as wall hangings.

## 6. WAFUKAN ICHI

9–2 Sanjo dori, Nakanocho,
Nakagyo-ku
211 8211
wafukan-ichi.jp
Mon–Sun 11am–8pm
[MAP 1 C3]

Wafukan Ichi specialises in furisode (a formal kimono), yukata (casual cotton kimonos) and hakama (pleated loose pants) that range from casual to very dressy. If you're in the market for a traditional Japanese outfit, newly made and with a cutting-edge contemporary design in vibrant colours, this store is a must-visit. If you're a fan of Japanese designer Tsumori Chisato, you'll certainly want to get yourself a kimono with a very modern Tsumori print from their WA collection. You can also grab a range of kimono accessories to give your outfit that extra special touch – the bags that come in thc Wafukan Ichi prints are highly coveted. Complete the look with modern tabi (split-toe) socks and geta (clogs/sandals) to match your kimono. If you're visiting around New Year's, ask about their prized grab bags.

**POCKET TIP**
Cat lovers can while away some time with new feline friends at cat cafe Wan Nyan Chu.

# 7. GALLERY KEI

671–1 Teramachi dori,
Kuenin, Maecho,
Nakagyo-ku
212 7114
http://gallerykei.jp
Mon–Sun 11.30am–6pm
[MAP 1 D1]

Passionate fabric hunter and collector Kawasaki Kei has put together a museum-level collection of vintage textiles and fabrics. The textures and dyes, the result of centuries of perfection, are miles away from the machine-made techno-fabric of today. Pieces are priced according to their age, rarity and intricacy, so you can pay over ¥3000 for an offcut. But every piece tells its own story, and prices aren't likely to faze textile purists in search of a piece of history. Noren (traditional fabric) curtains, festival-style matsuri (happi coats) and indigo-dyed fabrics hang on walls or sit in piles around the store, just waiting to be discovered. Kei themes her materials to create in-store exhibits, so it's a history lesson just walking through the doors.

# 8. KAMIJI KAKIMOTO

54 Teramachi dori, Tokiwagicho, Nakagyo-ku
211 3481
kyoto-kakimoto.jp
Mon–Sun 9am–6pm
[MAP 1 D1]

Japan is well known for its washi, or beautiful handmade paper. Craft capital Kyoto has spent years perfecting the art, and there's something about the quality and the tactile nature of the paper that makes it special. Established in 1845 in the late Edo period, Kakimoto is a focal point for crafters, folders, writers, and lovers of Japanese paper. Slide out the shelves and gasp at the breadth of colours, patterns, fibres and weaves. They specialise in yuzen, traditional hand-dyed paper, and kizuki-gami, which is made entirely from tree bark. All paper comes in different sizes, including popular small squares known as kaishi. Watch the staff show off their own paper-folding skills as they wrap your purchases in the Japanese diagonal wrapping style. Seasonal spins on stationery, writing pads and novelty items are also popular.

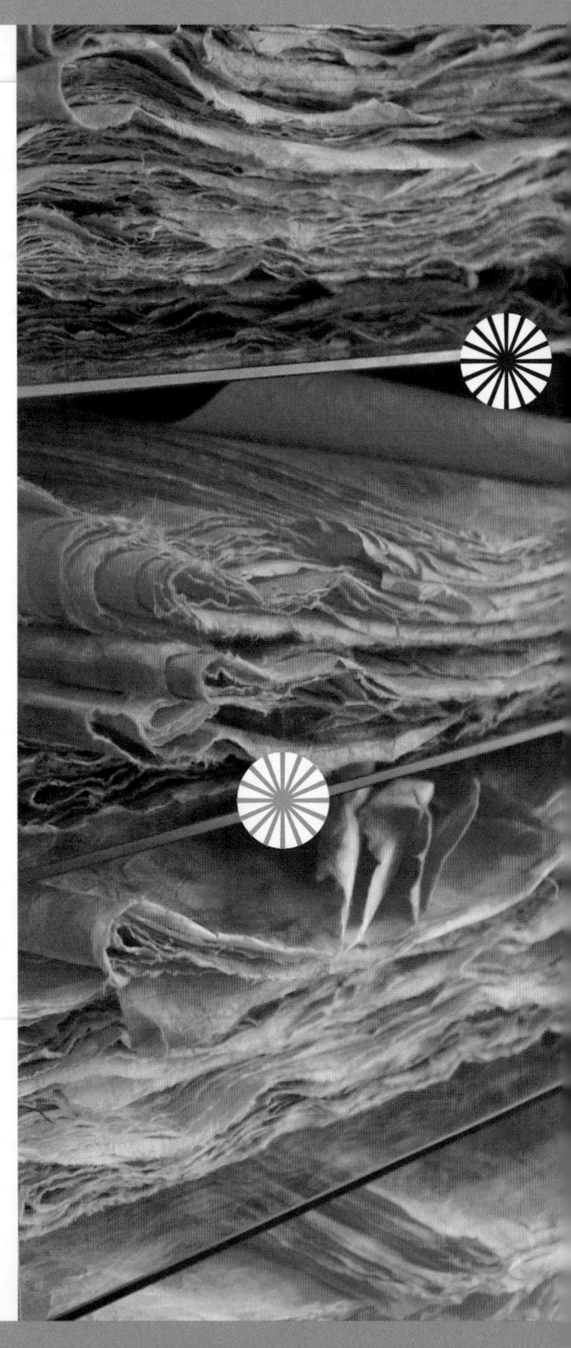

## 9. HAPPY JACK

224 Teramachi dori, Eirakucho,
Nakagyo-ku
213 3338
happyj.net
Mon–Sun 12am–8pm
[MAP 1 C3]

They play their music loud at Happy Jack. Record collectors passing by will automatically turn and climb the steep stairs to the third floor, like rats following the Pied Piper. The permanently hungover owner has used every square inch of the tiny space, and his collection of pre-loved mod and psychedelic vinyl, with a heavy nod to the 1960s, will have analogue devotees sifting through racks for hours. The Who feature heavily, of course – the store is named after one of their songs – but the Japanese pressings on 7-inch vinyl of French pop and soul are a highlight. The Japanese vinyl from the '60s through to the '80s is also great (check out the hair and shoulder pads). Elsewhere there's a good quota of rock, jazz, blues and the ubiquitous Beatles and Rolling Stones.

## 10. TERAMACHI SHOPPING

[MAP 1 D2]

Often called 'Craft Street' or 'Art Avenue', Teramachi dori is a street in two acts. Covered arcade **Shinkyogoku** is a popular strip with food joints, cheap and cheerful souvenirs, and the odd treasure. Picturesque **Horaido** is an old tea shop where genmaicha (brown rice tea) was invented. North Teramachi, across Nijo dori, is the top end, lined with long-standing paper, textiles, calligraphy and tea stores. Calligraphy buffs should head to **Kobaien**, where they have been making ink and brushes for more than 400 years. **Banterra** has an impressive range of goods made from bamboo or wood. **Kyoto Antique Centre** is a bazaar with many stores selling dolls, statuettes, temple bells, kimonos, ceramics and more. There's a pocket in the middle of Teramachi that is vintage heaven. **Poco a Poco** and **100000t alonetoco** have great used vinyl, CDs and books. For retro clothing, head into **Roger's** or **Small Change**. **Petit a Petit** sells printed fabric, while rubber stamp enthusiasts should head to **Tamaru Inbou**, who have been in the stamp business for more than a hundred years.

hundred years. They boast more than 2000 stamp designs, including historical characters, kanji, local animals and manga. Come on, you know you want that stamp of Monkey flying on a cloud! Built up an appetite? **Naruto Taiyaki Hompo** is a picturesque stall in the middle of Teramachi that sells piping hot fish-shaped waffles filled with red-bean paste or custard.

# 11. IPPODO

52 Teramachi dori, Tokiwagicho,
Nakagyo-ku
211 3421
ippodo-tea.co.jp
Mon–Fri 9am–6pm, tearoom
10am–6pm (last orders 5.30pm)
[MAP 1 D1]

Three centuries of selling tea 'blessed by mother nature' and picked in the fertile local tea fields has made Ippodo the most famous tea house in Kyoto. It's the quintessential Kyoto tea-shopping experience – even the elegant dark wooden exterior, with Ippodo's kanji namesake splashed over noren (traditional fabric) curtains, is iconic. Tea varieties are extensive (sencha, matcha, hojicha, genmaicha and more). Visit the cafe, where tea comes in a set with a seasonal sweet at around ¥700–¥1200. If you choose a sencha or bancha, it will arrive with a small teapot, three teacups and a timer. Phrases like 'tea leaves unravelling' and 'do not agitate' are bandied about. If you're curious about which teas are shade or open-field cultivated, book in for a tea class or tasting session. At Christmas, line up for their limited-edition New Year tea. Ippodo also sells teapots, whisks, cups and canisters, some of the finest gifts you'll find.

# 12. CAFE BIBLIOTEC HELLO

650 Nijo dori, Seimeicho,
Nakagyo-ku
231 8625
http://cafe-hello.jp
Mon–Sun 11.30am–12am
[MAP 1 C1]

A jungle sprouts over the exterior of Cafe Bibliotec Hello, a popular hangout for locals and visitors who want to grab a drink or a coffee and relax. Inside, the jungle continues – potted plants, palms, ferns and even a tree – adding a charming hint of Victorian-era greenhouse, albeit an open-plan one with mid-century furniture and ceramics. This place is all about repeat customers. Open wooden beams divide the two floors, and both levels have small libraries with a range of covetable design books. Those who are too busy to read sit at bench tables and tap away on laptops while sipping coffee. Head in for lunch or dinner – the chicken curry hits the spot, or grab a sandwich and munch along in time to '60s jazz and pop. They serve olives with your drinks here, cementing the '60s vibe. It makes for a super-cool bar in the heart of the action, and with beer and plum wine at around ¥600, the price is right.

**POCKET TIP**
If doughnuts don't take your fancy, try a caramel rusk.

## 13. HITSUJI

355–1 Tominokoji dori, Oicho, Nakagyo-ku
221 6534
Wed–Sat 11am–6pm
[MAP 1 C1]

Hitsuji is spoken about in whispers. The rustic texture, artisan look and feel, and surprising flavour combinations make for some of the finest doughnuts you'll find in Japan and bring locals back again and again. The focus here is on healthy and natural. The doughnuts are made from natural yeast and sprouted rice, which gives rise to the phrase 'breathing doughnuts'. Sweetened with fine Japanese sugar and treated with special care when rising the dough, these doughnuts will be among the lightest, fluffiest treats you've ever tasted. Flavours are inventive and tantalising – black tea and cream cheese, sweet potato and black sesame, pumpkin with chestnut and coconut – and they all come in under ¥250.

# 14. INODA COFFEE HONTEN

140 Sakaimachi dori, Doyucho,
Nakagyo-ku
241 0915
inoda-coffee.co.jp
Mon–Sun 7am–7pm
[MAP 1 C3]

Morning breakfast is a tricky business in Kyoto – good thing they have Inoda Coffee. Established in 1970, we can't decide if this Kyoto institution is old-world charm or retro timewarp – probably a bit of both. Look for the iconic red coffee pot logo and the blue-and-white room with the huge old coffee grinder, a great photo opportunity, depending on how many bicycles are stacked out the front. Inside, waiters and waitresses are sharply dressed in kissaten (coffee house) chic. Brown brick, dark wood and checked tablecloths will make you feel like you're at a chalet in the Swiss mountains. Join the morning crowds and order cotton-filtered coffee and Inoda's famous egg sandwiches (pictured at right). The coffee ranges from Columbian to café au lait and is served in Viennese goblet-style glasses. So step back in time for your daily fix. It's old school, which is why the new-school kids love it so much.

## 15. AB

Assist Bldg, Basement,
476 Teramachi dori,
Kamihonnojimaecho,
Nakagyo-ku
211 8580
japonica-cafe.com
Tues–Sun 11am–11pm
[MAP 1 C2]

Among the old-world craft emporiums and established family businesses on Teramachi, you'll find a cool contemporary downstairs bunker cafe where you can grab a great coffee or a local craft beer. After some intense shopping, the laid-back atmosphere and friendly staff make this the perfect place to refuel. A simple lunch and dinner menu of well-priced burgers, rice dishes and salads will hit the spot, and so will the coffee (rockstar coffee makers Clamp Coffee [*see* p. 140] provide the beans). Pop your head into AB record store, a small backroom space that sells jazz, hip hop, soul and grooves, and provides the soundtrack for the main room, especially at night when it transforms into a lively local bar. Careful – what seems like a late boozy lunch might end with you hitting a nonexistent dance floor somewhere between the tables and the bathrooms.

**POCKET TIP**
If you're into coffee AND the Beatles, check out nearby Hamukomama – a favourite haunt of John Lennon and Yoko Ono.

## 16. CHISOU INASEYA

93 Aburayacho,
Nakagyo-ku
255 7250
http://chisouinaseya.com
Mon–Sun 11.30am–2.30pm,
5–11pm
[MAP 1 C3]

Head down a tiny lane and into a charming slice of yesteryear. Chisou Inaseya is the kind of place you'll wish you had as your local, and the friendly service will make you feel like you come here every day. Lunch is a delicious bargain – a simple kaiseki bento (takeout) box with tasty free-range chicken and pickles at an 'I can't believe I'm eating in a place this beautiful at this price' kind of deal. Make sure to order up some sake. We asked for the waitress's choice, and she brought out two – the regional favourite and the oldest sake brewed in Kyoto. We picked one of each and she poured the drinks out of gigantic bottles. If you want to try kaiseki dining, they do a clean, seasonal dinner here that won't break the bank. At night it turns into a fabulous bar. Old beams, cushions and tatami (straw) mats, and sake of the highest quality – the perfect Kyoto drinking experience.

**POCKET TIP**

Immerse yourself in the warlord history at Honnoji-ji Temple on Teramachi dori.

## 17. HONKE OWARIYA

322 Kurumayacho dori,
Niomontsukinukecho,
Nakagyo-ku
231 3446
https://honke-owariya.co.jp/en
Sun–Mon 11am–7pm
[MAP 1 B2]

When monks in ancient Kyoto needed to refuel after a hard day of praying and meditating, Honke Owariya supplied the soba. People talk about visiting ancient temples, but have you ever eaten at a restaurant that's more than 500 years old? Step through the noren (traditional fabric) curtains into the small courtyard, where a tranquil Japanese garden sets the scene. Inside is an unmissable two-storey Japanese house from feudal times. Slip into one of the corner tables or scissor yourself down onto a tatami (straw) mat and sip sake while you think of all those who have been there before you. The houri soba set special, at ¥2160, is a pillar of fresh, chewy soba noodles with prawn tempura and an assortment of vegetables for dipping. There's an English menu to save us learning a 500-year-old dialect. Don't forget to grab one of their sweet rice cakes on the way out. Honke Owariya started out as a confectioner – so the sweets are older than the soba!

## 18. CAFE INDEPENDANTS

1928 Basement Bldg,
56 Sanjo dori, Benkeiishicho,
Nakagyo-ku
255 4312
cafe-independants.com
Mon–Sun 11.30–12am
[MAP 1 C3]

Viva la revolution! Housed in an old socialist meeting place, you can almost smell the ink and hear the talk of revolution at this uber-cool underground cafe and bar. It's a popular hangout for students and intellectuals who want to plot a coup while sipping craft beer, or write their manifesto on the back of a coaster. A cafe for the people, they do simple curries, pastas and burgers here, and there's an extensive list of European beer, which you can quaff in small booths or at bench tables. The walls of exposed brick and white beams seem to barely hold up the building – part of its rustic charm. Check out the side entrance with its dangerously steep stairs and peeling walls glued into place by old posters of Freddy Mercury, cowboy Elvis and pop graphics with revolutionary intent.

**POCKET TIP**
Check out cool Radio Cafe next door – they actually have their own radio station!

# 19. GYOZA CHAU CHAU

117 Kiyamachi dori, Ishiyacho, Nakagyo-ku
251 0056
gyozaya.com/chao
Mon–Thurs 5pm–1.30am, Fri 5pm–2.30am, Sat 2pm–2.30am, Sun 2pm–1.30am
[MAP 1 D3]

Gyoza Chau Chau was the Japan gyoza (dumplings) champion two years in a row, so you know it's good. Squeeze yourself into this rough-and-tumble eatery and grab a seat at the counter, where you can watch the gyoza being made. Join in the raucous conversation – the waiters will engage you from the start. Gyoza Chau Chau claims to have been 'supporting the salaryman since the '20s with peace of mind at a low price'. You'll feel the love – the perfectly crispy gyoza are seriously good. All gyoza are under ¥500, and happy-hour beers are dangerously cheap at ¥320. Vegetarians, rejoice – the tasty yuba gyoza (freeze-dried tofu wrapped with soy milk skin) and shiba zuke (stuffed with soy pulp and Kyoto-style pickles) are excellent. Leave enough room to order the chocolate gyoza for dessert!

# SOUTH HIGASHIYAMA

Ancient beauty and spectacular Buddhist treasures proudly perch on the slopes of Kyoto's eastern mountain range. The southern corner is one of the prime destinations for day trippers, a snap-happy wonderland of 'oohh' and 'aahh' moments with many places of enormous cultural significance. The amount of World Heritage–listed sights within walking distance is astounding.

South Higashiyama will be Day One for many visitors to Kyoto. Little is spoilt here and you're bound to be impressed by the abundance of beautiful shrines, gardens and walkways. Take a pilgrimage through the preserved streets of Ninen-zaka and Sanzen-zaka, and don't forget the ultimate destination – the stunning temple of Kyomizu-dera, standing proudly on its thick wooden stilts. South Higashiyama holds the key to Kyoto's combined power of iconic monuments and ancient Zen-like calm. There are also some not-to-be-missed shopping and eating secrets just a stone's throw from the action.

SIGHTS
1. Kiyomizu-dera
2. Kawai Kanjiro Memorial Museum
SHOPPING
3. Maiko Antiques
4. Uragu
5. Otsuka Gofukuten
SHOPPING AND EATING
6. Ten Cafe and Zakka
7. Ninen-zaka shopping
8. Sannen-zaka shopping
9. Matsubara dori
10. Fumon-an
EATING AND DRINKING
11. % Arabica Coffee
12. Tempura Endo
13. Yoshimura Kiyomizuan

# 1. KIYOMIZU-DERA

[MAP 1 G6]

Sitting proudly midway up the slopes of Mount Ottawa, Kiyomizu-dera is a Buddhist complex devoted to Kannon, the goddess of mercy. If the monks had ¥100 for every photograph taken here, they would surely be rich. The dark wooden main hall, teetering high on wooden pillars among the towering trees, is one of the most spectacular and vertigo-inducing things you'll ever see. Whether you go during cherry blossom season, the lush greenery of summer, the fading auburns of autumn, or the stark white snows of winter, Kiyomizu-dera well and truly lives up to its status as the most visited place in Kyoto. Make sure you stop by the Otowa no taki waterfall and sip from the mountain water – it's thought to have life-prolonging properties.

**POCKET TIP**

The spectacular Sanjusangendo is a must. Find your face among the 1000 Kannon statues and have good luck!

**KIYOMIZU-DERA**
294 Kiyomizu 1-chome
Higashiyama-ku
Bus no 100, 206
Mon–Sun 6am, closing time varies

**KAWAII KANJIRO MEMORIAL MUSEUM**
569 Kaneicho, Higashiyama-ku
Bus no 202, 206
Tues–Sun 10am–5pm

## 2. KAWAI KANJIRO MEMORIAL MUSEUM

[MAP 1 E7]

Kawai Kanjiro, the famed folk-art ceramicist of the early 1900s, lived and worked in this house. Anyone into sculpture or ceramics should put this on their 'must do' list. If you're into Japanese architecture you might just visit for the house, a beautiful old machiya (traditional wooden townhouse) with dark and light wood walls and floors, and shoji screens opening onto tranquil gardens. Pay the ¥900 entrance fee, take off your shoes and put on the slippers provided – this is sacred ground, and not to be scraped and scuffed by clumsy feet. Kanjiro's modernist influences shine through, and as you stroll through the stunning rooms, each exhibiting aspects of Kanjiro's art, you can sense how the artist lived and worked. Eventually, you will arrive outside to marvel at the impressive eight-chambered kiln where Kanjiro fired his creations.

## 3. MAIKO ANTIQUES

157 Komatsucho,
Higashiyama-ku
541 2626
http://maikoantiques.strikingly.com
Sat–Sun 1–6pm, irregular hours on weekdays
[MAP 1 D5]

Maiko Antiques has one of the most oddball collections of Showa era (1926–1989) vintage treasures. Start by riffling through the stuff out the front – the evocative samurai postcards will have you rethinking your haircut, while pre-loved yukatas (casual cotton kimonos) and kimonos will complete the look. Once inside, you may wish to inform your nearest and dearest that you'll be uncontactable for hours. Kewpie dolls, freaky masks, matchboxes, old lanterns, books, boxes, tins and toys compete for space on overstuffed shelves. It's hard to believe anyone let the amazing black-and-white photographs go. Blush at the large range of geisha porn figurines – you're sure to learn a thing or two. Elsewhere, orthotic limbs or false teeth offer a touch of the bizarre – if you're planning to start your own creepy science museum you'll find some prime exhibits here. Opening hours vary during the week, so check the website.

**POCKET TIP**
Keep a lookout on this street for geisha going about their business.

# 4. URAGU

297 Miyagawasuji 4-chome,
Higashiyama-ku
551 1357
uragu.com
Tues–Sun 12–6pm
[MAP 1 D5]

Letter writers, stationery obsessives and calligraphers will delight in Uragu, a hidden gem in the picturesque backstreets that puts a modern spin on traditional Kyoto craft. Find the discreet circular sign, wander down the thin cobblestone path, through the noren (traditional fabric) curtains and into a 100-year-old machiya (traditional wooden townhouse) that exquisitely displays artfully arranged artisan paper products. The paper is pure and simple, and designs are a modern take on the classics applied with a delicate touch. Stock up on beautiful kotomori message cards, delicate envelopes and the mameno notepad, a pad that resembles a tiny box.

## 5. OTSUKA GOFUKUTEN

88–1, Hoshinocho,
Higashiyama-ku
533 0533
otsuka-gofukuten.jp
Mon–Sun 11am–7pm
[MAP 1 F5]

Traditional Kyoto is getting a contemporary makeover. Otsuka Gofukuten are at the forefront, evolving the classic kimono into a modern style of dress for the Kyoto-ite on the go. Their three-step price system, from casual to sophisticated, will give you room to move. With kimonos in contemporary checks and stripes and updates on more traditional patterns, it's a safe bet that whether you want to wear your kimono shopping or out to dinner, there will be something here for you. Why not pair your modern kimono with one of their capes? Add footwear from the range of geta (sandals, pictured at right) in surprisingly bold colours. Accessories including umbrellas and handbags will tie your new look together.

## 6. TEN CAFE AND ZAKKA

208–10 Matusubara dori,
Kiyomizu 2-chrome,
Higashiyama-ku
533 6252
http://ten.higoyomi.com
Tues–Sun 9.30am–7pm
[MAP 1 F6]

Ten Cafe and Zakka has a standout range of work from local makers. The happy, waving bear on the white noren (traditional fabric) flag ushers you in to find a range of covetable local ceramics. Check out Toru Yamashita's mid-century-influenced pottery. Beautifully packaged incense, tenugui (hand towels), furoshiki (traditional wrapping cloth) and some of the best vintage noren curtains line the walls and shelves. While your purchases are being wrapped, head into the cafe for a quick coffee and matcha cheesecake, or some homemade ginger ale, and watch the masses as they file past the window on their way to **Kiyomizu-dera** (*see* p. 72).

**POCKET TIP**

You can't miss Yasaka-no-to Pagoda. Head inside – unlike most other pagodas in Kyoto, you can climb this one!

# 7. NINEN-ZAKA SHOPPING

[MAP 1 F6]

Leave your uncomfortable shoes at home – this crooked, cobbled laneway from centuries past cuts a path across South Higashiyama and is one of the most walked (and shopped) streets in Kyoto. Get a maiko makeover at **Shiki** or shop for local Gosho dolls at the **Shimada Koen** doll workshop. Shop for incense at **Niimi** and rub shoulders with girlfriends dressed for the occasion in yukatas (casual cotton kimonos), buying popular bear-head drum toys or kokeshi dolls and other fun souvenirs. Specialty food stalls are everywhere. Taste some fresh umeboshin (pickled plums perfect for any Samurai snack pack) at **Ousuno sato**. If you're hungry there are plenty of stores selling roasted crackers or dango (dumplings) on skewers – perfect walking food. When you're tired, head into atmospheric tea house **Kasagiya**, located on the stone steps that lead to the Sannen-zaka path. The entryway, with its hanging blue flag and weathered wood, holds a tiny tea room with small tables, cushions and bamboo pillars. Try the towering green matcha kakigori (shaved ice dessert) or the red bean frappe.

**POCKET TIP**
To avoid the tourist crush, hit the streets early morning or late afternoon/evening.

# 8. SANNEN-ZAKA SHOPPING

[MAP 1 F6]

Steep, winding Sannen-zaka leads to **Kiyomizu-dera** (*see* p. 72) and, like its sibling Ninen-zaka, it's brimming with old-world charm and unique shopping opportunities. Rumour is that Sannen-zaka is cursed, so shake the jinx with a gourd or maneki-neko (lucky cat) from talisman specialist store **Hyotan-ya**. For a more traditional take on incense, head into **Shoyeido**. The tiny scented pouches make great gifts. For a sweet stop, head into popular **Rakusyu** and tuck into a towering matcha parfait or their specialty Kusa warabi-mochi, green tea-covered bracken starch dumplings. **Inoda Coffee Honten** (*see* p. 64) has an outlet here housed in a stylish mid-century building. With stores selling kitchenalia, cat-related products, noren (traditional fabric) curtains, sake vessels and more, it's a trinket hunter's dream.

# 9. MATSUBARA DORI

[MAP 1 F6]

Matsubara dori is a riot of colourful stalls, shops and stands selling some of the most varied mixes of local street food you're likely to find. You won't know where to start, or when to stop, as you make your way from savoury to sweet and back again. Munch on a pickled cucumber on a stick covered in matcha powder (iced in summer), or the popular yatsuhashi – rice-flour triangles flavoured with cinnamon or stuffed with red-bean paste. Try the delicious, glutinous namafu dengaku squares, grilled over an open flame. Graze on all manner of roasted rice crackers, pickles, green-tea roll cake and the ever-popular soft-serve ice-cream. Our favourite flavour is black sesame, but take your pick from matcha, brown rice, soy (vegan), barley, roasted tea, buckwheat noodle or even cheese biscuit! Get in early for the purple sweet potato, as it sells out fast. Wash down steamed meat buns with Asahi or a green juice. Healthy options include green smoothies or yuzu (a type of citrus fruit) and shiso juice. You can even buy cherry blossoms pickled in salt. This is Kyoto fast food from times gone by – chances are you've never seen anything like it.

**POCKET TIP**

Stay hydrated on your temple walk with a cold or hot vending-machine green tea.

"DRY"
Asahi

580円
780
10個入 540円
サンプル ケースを押さないで！割れます
夏
生八ツ橋
9個入(各3個) 540円
¥650
京都

ビタミンCがいっぱい
冷た〜い
抹茶ティー
一杯 200円

冷
漬物まるかぶり
ひやっこい胡瓜
一本
250円

## 10. FUMON-AN

264–2 Kiyomizu 2-chrome,
Higashiyama-ku
533 8282
http://fumon-an.co.jp
Mon–Sun 10am–5.30pm
[MAP 1 F6]

A tiny lane off the main drag leads down to a store with a serious sweet tooth. This is Candyland, but not as you know it. If you're new to Kyoto sweet flavours, it's all here, under a giant bobbing lantern sporting the Fumon-an logo. Tastings are liberal – try the warabi-mochi (powdered sweet jelly; not for everyone, but quite addictive) or the tasty red-bean cakes. Soft serve is a specialty. The matcha flavours here are extracted from the first tea leaves of the season, the ichiban cha, so you know they're good. The packaging is beautiful, all with the signature logo. Staff will let you know the use-by date, though you'll probably already have the sweets in your mouth. Take a seat at the back of the cafe on the logo cushion and look out onto the mini-garden as you inhale your sweets, or head into the cafe next door for some seriously dangerous parfaits with tiny wafers which, surprisingly, have the cute store logo on them.

**POCKET TIP**

Arabica also has a super cute Arashiyama coffee shack and a pop-up in Fuji Daimaru (*see* p. 32).

## 11. % ARABICA COFFEE

87 Hoshinocho,
Higashiyama-ku
746 3669
arabica.coffee
Mon–Sun 8am–6pm
[MAP 1 F5]

If you worship at the shrine of coffee, duck into Arabica on the way up to **Kiyomizu-dera** (*see* p. 72) for a shot of some of the city's finest brews. Languishing under the gaze of spectacular **Yasaka-no-to Pagoda**, Arabica is light-years away from the old-world feel of the area. Strikingly clean lines, concrete and glass and the 'per cent' logo are all new-school additions to the landscape, yet somehow they manage to capture the handcrafted feel of the south-east. Coffee snobs from Melbourne to Portland will give them the thumbs-up. Beans are roasted on site and are single origin. Arabica clearly love what they do – baristas include Yuka, an ex-maiko (apprentice geisha) who chose the way of the bean, and latte art champion Junichi Yamaguchi. Their dedication to high-quality coffee brings locals and visitors flocking. For those who can't get going without a coffee hit, it's open from eight in the morning.

## 12. TEMPURA ENDO

566 Yasaka dori, Komatsucho,
Higashiyama-ku
551 1488
gion-endo.com
Mon–Sun 11.30am–3pm,
5–10pm
[MAP 1 E5]

Tempura devotees, it's time to take it to the next level. Tempura Endo is one of the world's most highly regarded restaurants. It's set up in an incredible 90-year-old tea house, once home to geiko and maiko (geisha). At ¥10,000–¥15,000 for dinner (splash out on the ¥18,000 special), it's certainly an indulgence, but lunchtime is ¥4000–¥8000 – a bargain for this memorable experience. The expertly fried, crispy tempura is embellished with seasonal opulence. You'll have the chance to experience some very flavourful tempura delicacies, like the specialty corn tempura or the sea urchin wrapped in dried seaweed. Sit at the counter and watch the masters at work – each delicate piece will be placed before you like a precious gift. You can stalk the Tempura Endo website from the time you book to the time you arrive and put together your fantasy menu. As an added bonus for those seeking calm indulgence, no kids are allowed. If you can't get a booking, pick up some boxed tempura rice rolls to take away.

# 13. YOSHIMURA KIYOMIZUAN

208–9 Matsubara dori,
Kiyomizu 2-chrome,
Higashiyama-ku
533 1212
http://arashiyama-yoshimura.com/kiyomizu
Mon–Sun 11am–5pm
[MAP 1 F6]

A contemporary noodle restaurant that prides itself on making noodles by hand, Yoshimura Kiyomizuan provides a welcome respite from the crowds of shoppers on Matsubara dori. The exterior is opulent; precious white noren (traditional fabric) curtains (pictured above) over the beautiful old building usher you into a picturesque room where the premium service belies the touristy nature of the area. The buckwheat noodles are fresh, chewy and perfect in hot soup with tempura or cold with dipping sauce, both well priced at around ¥1500. Request a window seat for a beautiful view of the mountains. Order frothy draft beer (it comes in amazing ceramic mugs) or be daring and try the unusual and potent soba cooking water mixed with shochu (distilled sweet potato spirit). Careful getting up, though – this drink sneaks up on you. Investigate their range of picnic boxes and takeaway desserts if you feel like lunch in the mountains.

**POCKET TIP**
Climb the hill to Chionin. Sit cross-legged, pick up a stick and make music with the bells.

# GION

As you cross Shijo Bridge and the grand Kabuki Theatre comes into view, you'll find yourself floating into the heart of Gion, gateway to the mountains and many of Kyoto's most popular temples and shrines. Shut your eyes and you'll be transported into Kyoto's rich and golden past, where geisha and maiko (apprentice geisha) rushed from one appointment to the next, well-to-do families shopped for the most exquisite products, and small stores perfected their craft.

Old-time Japanese sweet shops sit alongside galleries, museums, long-held family businesses and shops that have serviced Kyoto for hundreds of years. The action is centred around Shijo dori and popular Hanamikoji dori, but slip down the side streets for quieter Kyoto moments. Clever brands have set up shop in the most beautiful and picturesque laneways, bringing a new wave of savvy shoppers to the area.

Spend an afternoon combing the side streets for independent stores selling antiques, books and curiosities. Sit down to a lunch of perfectly formed sushi or while away the afternoon with tea and Japanese sweets. Amazing food and shopping opportunities all add to a quintessential Kyoto experience.

SIGHTS
1. Hanamikoji dori
2. Minamiza Kabuki Theatre
SHOPPING
3. Yojiya
4. Kazurasei
5. Leica Store Kyoto
6. Books & Things
SHOPPING AND EATING
7. Pass the Baton
8. Sfera
9. Malebranche Cacao 365
EATING AND DRINKING
10. Mametora
11. Oku
12. Gion Yuki

# 1. HANAMIKOJI DORI

[MAP 1 E4]

If you listen closely, you can hear echoes of the geisha in their geta sandals clip-clopping from one appointment to another along the cobbled streets in days of old – or maybe it's the real thing. Today, you're sure to see a geisha or maiko (apprentice geisha) getting into a taxi or hopping onto a Japanese rickshaw. You're in Kyoto's heartland here: picture postcard–preserved machiya (traditional wooden townhouses), cobbled streets, noren (traditional fabric) curtains and beautiful lanterns. Ochaya (tea houses) still perform the traditional tea ceremony, and machiya are home to restaurants that excel in kaiseki cuisine. With delicate, refined food, dessert houses, traditional shops and a vast range of souvenirs, this is the Kyoto you've dreamt of. For an introduction into the arts that have defined Gion, book into 'The Culture Show', where real maiko in training demonstrate the tea ceremony, ikebana (flower arranging), Bunraku puppet theatre, kyo-mai dance and the koto zither in an hour-long show at **Yasaka Hall** on Gion Corner.

**HANAMIKOJI DORI**
Gionmachi Minamigawa, Higashiyama-ku
Gojo Station (Heien Line) or bus no 46

**MINAMIZA KABUKI THEATRE**
198 Shijo dori, Nakanocho, Higashiyama-ku
Gojo Station (Heien Line) or bus no 46
Times vary

## 2. MINAMIZA KABUKI THEATRE

[MAP 1 E4]

As you cross Shijo Bridge into Gion it's hard to miss the striking building commanding some major real estate on your right. This stately, ornate facade, with its gabled roof, is the **Minamiza**, the main Kyoto destination for one of Japan's most famous arts: a highly stylised drama called kabuki theatre. This striking form of theatre is both captivating and beguiling – all part of its charm. Comical, tragic, high art and low art in rapid succession, kabuki is like opera: musical theatre and farce, with a hefty dose of make-up and costumes that continues to inspire many of the great western fashion houses. Performances can cost anywhere from ¥4200 to ¥27,000, so be sure to check the price before you book. If you're not keen on theatre, pop in and have a look around the building anyway. It was built in 1929 to house a theatre company that's thought to go back as far as 1610.

## 3. YOJIYA

Shijo dori, Goinmachi, Kitagawa, Higashiyama-ku
541 0177
yojiya.co.jp
Mon–Sun 10am–8pm
[MAP 1 E4]

The iconic image of a woman's face reflected in her hand mirror looms over this famous Kyoto cosmetic shop. The Gion branch of Yojiya was the first, founded in 1904. The brand originally catered to the geisha's particular needs, and you may still find yourself shopping next to a plain-clothes geisha, alongside beauty-obsessed elite and everyday Kyoto-ites alike. The go-to product is blotting paper, which removes harmful oils without ruining your make-up. It comes in portable, handy packs perfect for travellers. You can also buy soap, hand cream, lip gloss and make-up accessories, all in Yojiya's tasteful packaging and at a great price point. A Kyoto institution, Yojiya is an unmissable Gion shopping experience.

## 4. KAZURASEI

285 Shijo dori, Goinmachi,
Kitagawa,
Higashiyama-ku
561 0672
kazurasei.co.jp
Mon–Sun 10am–7pm,
closed Wed
[MAP 1 E4]

While the mysteries of the geisha may be impenetrable, you can at least shop like a geisha at Kazurasei. Yin to Yojiya's Yang, Kazurasei keeps a lower profile, but is just as prized. This shop is old-school Gion and has been serving the local geisha since 1865, making sure their hair is immaculate. Kazurasei stocks hair accessories – check out the boxwood combs and ornamental lacquer hairpins, some which look like they belong in a museum (and are priced accordingly). The holy grail here is the magical hair balm, tsubaki oil, made from the prized camellia nut. At around ¥3000 for a small bottle, it's worth the investment. This magical elixir has kept geisha hair beautiful for hundreds of years. Now you, too, can share in this beauty secret, which locals swear by. The oil also features in shampoos and skin care products. If you're prone to dry lips you might want to pick up some of their honey and safflower lip balm.

**POCKET TIP**
You'll find lots of Japanese sweet shops and dessert cafes in and around Gion's main streets.

# 5. LEICA STORE KYOTO

570–120 Hanamikoji dori,
Gionmachi Minamigawa,
Higashiyama-ku
532 0320
leica-camera.com
Tues–Sun 11am–7pm
[MAP 1 E5]

Duck under the noren (traditional fabric) curtains to enter the low-lit, atmospheric Leica flagship store. Camera buffs will flip – Leica Camera AG is an internationally operating manufacturer of cameras and sport optics, and the display makes this store seem more like a museum. Here, German precision merges with Kyoto craft – the 100-year-old, two-storey townhouse has been refashioned into a store you won't find the likes of anywhere in the world. The original frontage and reused beams and pillars hold the house's memories intact, and the contemporary rework goes hand-in-hand with the cameras' timeless design. Leica enthusiasts will savour the limited-edition products and collaborations with local artisans. Upstairs you'll find a beautiful gallery featuring exhibitions by world-renowned photographers. Oh, and the cameras are duty free, if that helps you afford one.

## 6. BOOKS & THINGS

375–5 Motomachi,
Higashiyama-ku
744 0555
http://andthings.exblog.jp
Mon–Sun 12–7pm
[MAP 1 E3]

If you're on the hunt for a 1960s treatise on modernism or an out-of-print Picasso biography, you're likely to find it at Books & Things. In-the-know book hunters seek out this intimate space, housed in an old machiya (traditional wooden townhouse) down a mysterious narrow alleyway. You'll have to slip off your shoes – the tatami (straw) mat floors are still intact, and shoji screens continue the traditional theme. This is small-scale retail done with love and passion. Owner Kojima Yasutsugu has made the space his haven, a home away from home. You half expect him to decide at the last minute that he doesn't want to part with the book you've chosen. This is a secret that bibliophiles will want to keep to themselves – analogue, independent shopping that will delight young shoppers and take older ones back to a simpler time.

**POCKET TIP**
Explore Gion's backstreets and tiny alleyways.

# 7. PASS THE BATON

77–6 Sueyoshicho,
Higashiyama-ku
708 3668
pass-the-baton.com
Mon–Sat 11am–8pm,
Sun 11am–7pm
[MAP 1 E4]

Tokyo's Pass the Baton deals in quirky and hard-to-find vintage treasures. This magical pocket of Gion is the perfect location for the store's aesthetic, with its bending willow trees and crumbling houses overlooking the Shirakawa River. A charming bridge deposits you at a repurposed 120-year-old machiya (traditional wooden townhouse). Inside, the steel-and-glass display with hanging lanterns harkens back to the past while simultaneously bringing the store into the present. You'll find an ecclectic collection of kimonos, toys and vintage oddities. From the beautiful to the bizarre, you never know what you'll get. Everything is unique and original, supporting the store's credo 'appreciate what already exists and create new value'. It's reinvigorated the area too: the cool Tokyo kids have set up shop here and the Kyoto kids are going nuts for it. Stop for a drink or an outrageous honey chai shaved ice (¥1200) at their tea and sake room, **Tasuki**, which overlooks the gently flowing river.

## 8. SFERA

17 Yamato Oji dori,
Benzaitencho,
Higashiyama-ku
532 1105
ricordi-sfera.com/en/shops
Thurs–Tues 11am–7pm,
bar Mon–Sat 7pm–4am
[MAP 1 E3]

Not far from the heart of traditional Gion you'll find Sfera, a contemporary design store that adopts the devotion to quality handcrafted products that Kyoto is famous for, and updates it for the Now. Beautiful one-off ceramics, tea caddies, fans, porcelain and cutlery sit on the shelves like precious gallery exhibits. Choose between numerous handmade designs – the slight imperfections in each object make them unique, so pick one that suits your personality. The kitchenware here will have you mentally upgrading your own space. Downstairs, you'll find a workspace and a cafe. Say hello to super-cute French bulldog Don (pictured above). He might ignore you, though – he's famous now that he's the face of DOnG, his own range of pet products. If you're in the area at night, make sure you check out **Satonaka** on the third floor, a new take on a Kyoto bar where they serve drinks in Sfera's designer glassware.

# 9. MALEBRANCHE CACAO 365

570–150 Gionmachi,
Minamigawa,
Higashiyama-ku
551 6060
malebranche.co.jp
Wed–Mon 10am–6pm
[MAP 1 E4]

Malebranche is the number one destination for Kyoto-ites looking to pick up a gift. Exquisite packaging and delicate flavours are east meets west and traditional meets modern. In a quiet, narrow street just off Hanamikoji you'll find their secret weapon, a destination store for chocoholics. Head through the noren (traditional fabric) flags into this delightful remodelled machiya (traditional wooden townhouse), the perfect setting for a sweet splurge. People queue up for the delicious 'Langue de Chat', or cat's tongue biscuits. The chocolate wagashi (sweets) are like tiny jewels, too beautiful to eat – almost. On hot days a matcha chocolate ice-cream (pictured at right) is the perfect way to cool down. A stunningly wrapped box of Malebranche chocolates or biscuits makes for the perfect Kyoto gift. The temptation to eat the gift will be great, so maybe buy two.

## 10. MAMETORA

570–235 Gionmachi,
Minamigawa,
Higashiyama-ku
532 3955
kiwa-group.co.jp/restaurant/196
Mon–Sun 11.30am–2pm, 5–9pm
[MAP 1 E5]

Mametora is a beautiful machiya (traditional wooden townhouse) on Hanamikoji dori where they serve a world-famous version of mamezushi, Kyoto's unique style of sushi. Often referred to as maiko sushi, the size and shape is perfect for the 'button-shaped' mouths of the apprentice geisha. Downstairs, small private rooms spill off a lantern-lit hallway. Upstairs, the room is the epitome of traditional beauty, with old-school artworks and ikebana (flower arranging). The fantastically priced set gives you a glimpse of the majesty of kaiseki cuisine. At ¥4200 for a five-course set meal, including a jewel box mamezushi set, it's a traditional Gion experience that you will treasure. The precious jewel box features artfully arranged mackerel, shrimp, bamboo shoots, squid, pickled tuna, ginger and more, placed delicately in wooden boxes that make you feel like you're receiving a tray of precious gems. It's all a work of art, and the clientele are dressed accordingly. If you want the full kaiseki experience, it is available at dinner time only and will set you back around ¥10,000.

## 11. OKU

570–119 Gionmachi,
Minamigawa,
Higashiyama-ku
531 4776
oku-style.com
Wed–Mon 11.30am–9pm
[MAP 1 E4]

There's something special about the quiet side streets of Hanamikoji. Head into the tranquil lanes and look for the purple banner with the rising sun over Mount Fuji. Once inside, you'll find Oku, a contemporary designer space overlooking a small Japanese garden that speaks to both the old and the new. Famed chef Hisato Nakahigashi uses Oku to test out his new experiments with local produce. Kaiseki-themed lunch sets are artfully arranged and come in around ¥2800 for grilled fish, tofu and seasonal side dishes. A wafer and ice-cream dessert is an added bonus. The Kaiseki dinner, at around ¥38,000, is a steal for this part of town. At night, Oku transforms into an atmospheric bar. Don't fight history – pop in and drink where many workers, businessmen and geisha have drunk before you.

## 12. GION YUKI

111–1 Tominagacho,
Higashiyama-ku
525 2666
Mon–Fri 5–10.30pm,
Sat 5–11.30pm
[MAP 1 E4]

When the sun goes down, after you've shopped 'til you dropped and snapped endless pics of sublime temples, it's time to pretend you're not a tourist. Make like a local and head to Gion Yuki. This gritty, no-nonsense izakaya (gastropub) is your one-stop shop for booze and food – a smoky, authentic eatery that draws crowds of rowdy locals. Expect to line up for their grilled scallops, fried eggplant and assorted vegetable dishes. The sashimi here is seriously good. Wash it down with some local beer or sake. Grab a seat overlooking the manic kitchen, where chefs are framed by eye-catching red banners covered in recipes written in kanji. You'll be flanked by chatty workers, regulars and old-timers, worlds away from the tourist-filled eateries.

# NORTH HIGASHIYAMA

As you head further north, the mountain air fills your lungs, the scenery becomes more arresting and the atmosphere is tranquil and leisurely. This is the Kyoto we go home and dream about. Beautiful temples and shrines are no less plentiful, but with more destinations off the tourist bus route, chances are you'll find yourself alone in some of the most beautiful places on Earth.

From peaceful Zen Buddhist temple Nanzen-ji you can walk in quiet contemplation, as locals and monks have for many years, along the Philosopher's Path, a prime viewing spot for cherry blossoms. The path takes you to the popular Ginkakuji (Silver Temple) and its perfectly manicured gardens.

North Higashiyama is also where you'll find the towering vermillion tori gate that leads to the Heian Shrine, whose garden is home to the stepping stones made famous by a contemplative Scarlett Johansson in *Lost in Translation*. Wander through the maze-like temple complex of Chion-in, and head up the impossibly steep stairs to find the melancholy temple of bells and a peaceful cemetery. The panoramic view of Kyoto is an added bonus. Over the past five years a contemporary shopping and cafe scene has surprised temple-goers with an eclectic mix of old- and new-school wares.

SIGHTS
1. Nanzen-ji
2. Heian Shrine
3. The Philosopher's Path and Ginkakuji
SHOPPING
4. Kiso Artech
5. Artbooks Yamazaki
6. Tsunesaburo Lacquerware
SHOPPING AND EATING
7. Tsutaya Okazaki
8. Yojiya Cafe
EATING AND DRINKING
9. Unité
10. Omen
11. Mo-An

# 1. NANZEN-JI

[MAP 1 G3]

Nanzen-ji's Zen Buddhist roots date back to the 13th century. As head temple of the Rinzai sect, it has great cultural significance. The light at Nanzen-ji seems different, dappled and suffused through giant, whispering trees, illuminating patches of the greenest moss. It's hard to take a bad picture here – the majesty of the **Sanmon gate** and its thick, dark wood pillars are a photographer's dream. If the weather is right you can climb to the top of the gate for a breathtaking view of the surrounding woodlands. Pose for pics in the arches of the strangely out of place Meiji-period aqueduct (pictured at right). Buy an incense stick, plant it in the ash cauldron and feel the zen. And whatever you do, don't miss the moss-covered side garden, **Nanzen-in**, with its picturesque lake, stepping stones and tearoom. Northern garden **Hojo** mirrors natural forms, and the rocks are said to mimic tigers crossing the water. Dusk at Nanzen-ji, when the monastery bells start to toll, is an unforgettable experience.

**NANZEN-JI**
86 Nanzenji, Fukuchicho, Sakyo-ku
Keage Station or bus no 5
Mon–Sun 9am–5pm

**HEIAN SHRINE**
Okazaki, Nishitennoucho, Sakyo-ku
Higashiyama Station or bus no 5,100
Mon–Sun 6am–5.30pm (closing time varies by season)

## 2. HEIAN SHRINE

[MAP 1 G1]

Heian, a Shinto shrine, was built in 1895 to celebrate Kyoto's 1100th birthday. The garden is open from 6am, so if you want to avoid tourist crowds that's a good time to start. Spend a reflective day stepping lithely over the artfully arranged stones that were the breakout stars of Scarlett Johansson's reflective scene in *Lost in Translation*. There's a small fee to get into the garden, but in most seasons the covered bridge across the lake is a great place to sit and contemplate the beauty of nature. Look for the rare golden soft shell turtles that live here. There's also talk of an albino turtle, and a turtle with a coat of algae that looks like a straw raincoat – spot the latter and your luck will be on the rise. Like Narcissus, you can gaze at your image in the shimmering waterways, or watch the koi as they flitter about, swimming through canals and around tiny Crane and Turtle islands. In the south garden alone there are more than 200 kinds of plants, but the cherry blossoms reign supreme.

# 3. THE PHILOSOPHER'S PATH AND GINKAKUJI

[MAP 1 G1]

Whether you're planning your next great work or just contemplating life, a peaceful stroll alongside the moss-adorned canal of the Philosopher's Path will get your creative juices flowing. The great Japanese thinker Nishida Kitaro used to walk here during his meditations, so prime your antennae and get ready to receive inspiration. Crowds may block your transmission in cherry blossom season, so tread the path in the early morning or at fading light. Ginkakuji, also known as the Silver Temple, sits at the northern end of the walk. Dating back to 1482, the retirement villa of shogun Ashikaga Yoshimasa was meant to be silver plated, but he sadly ran out of funds. The temple is now known for its beautiful moss garden, breathtaking view and rather unique 'dry sand' garden (pictured at right), complete with a giant sand cone known delightfully as the 'moon viewing platform'. The wonderful **Togudo** building arguably outshines the Silver Temple itself. ¥500 will get you in.

## 4. KISO ARTECH

43 Shishigatani, Honenincho, Sakyo-ku
751 7175
http://kiso-artech.co.jp
Mon–Sun 9.30am–5.30pm
[MAP 1 G1]

Kiso Artech have added their quiet beauty to the Philosopher's Path – the perfect place for a store that prides itself on the most immaculate craftsmanship. The name comes from the merging of art, technology and the famed Japanese cypress from the Kiso mountains. The woodcraft is impeccable – delicate shoehorns, impossibly light wooden cups, handmade Edobitsu rice holders and rough-hewn chopping boards are all formed lovingly from 'Kiso Hinoki' and other local timbers. Their range of lacquerware and ceramics is the epitome of a refined Japanese aesthetic. The building mirrors the quality: a modern Japanese exterior overlooks the flowing canal and channels the zen atmosphere of Higashiyama. The interior displays reflect the surrounding beauty of the seasons – berries and seed-pods are strewn about, bringing the outside in. An unmissable diversion, Kiso Artech sell exquisite objects that will 'elegantly decorate' any living space.

## 5. ARTBOOKS YAMAZAKI

91–18 Okazaki, Enshojicho,
Sakyo-ku
762 0249
artbooks.jp
Tues–Sun 10am–6pm
[MAP 1 G2]

Hidden down a residential side street, Artbooks Yamazaki is a must for bibliophiles. Slip off your shoes and enter a magical, mystical world of old relics, parchments, scrolls and rare Japanese woodblock prints. The musty rooms with low wooden beams are crammed to the rafters with tomes from times gone by. Blow dust off weighty volumes and carefully unravel crumbling rolls of paper – just beware of picking up something thinking it's ¥10,000 only to find out that it's ¥100,000. Some of the items here are practically museum pieces. Scrounge around, though, and you might find a significantly old cartoon or illustrated book for a good price. You'll feel like a scholar or a treasure hunter uncovering long-lost ancient texts, and when you get it home you'll be amazed that you own a tiny slice of Kyoto's written history.

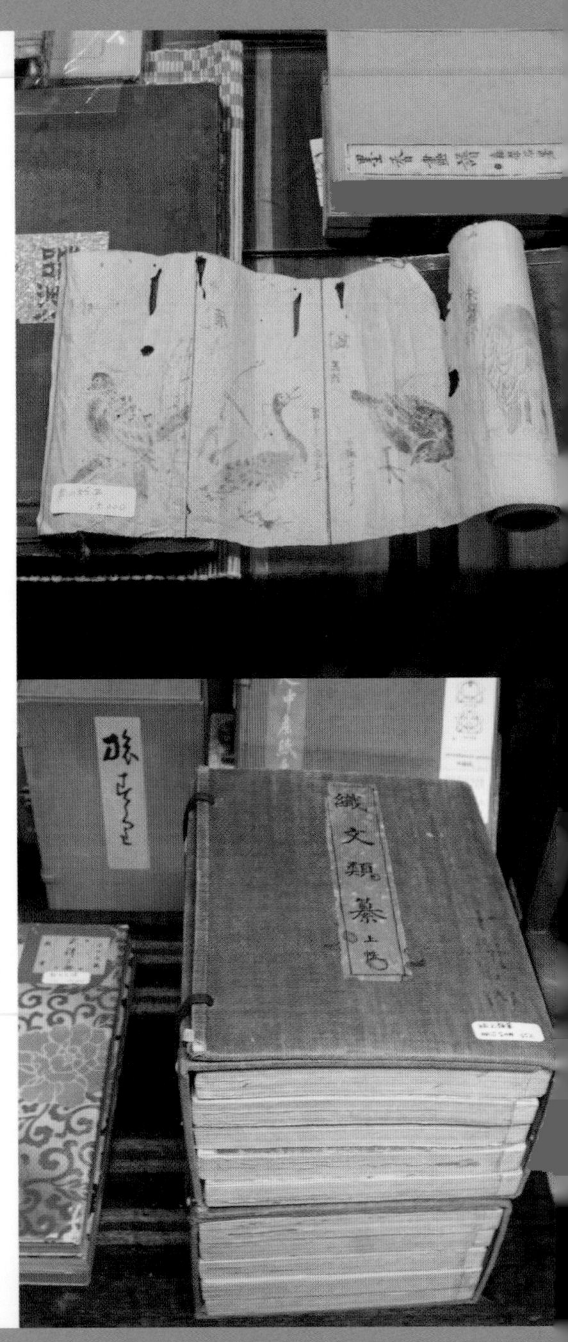

## 6. TSUNESABURO LACQUERWARE

151–1 Nishimachi,
Higashiyama-ku
771 6262
urushinotsunesaburo-w.com
Mon–Sun 10am–6pm
[MAP 1 G3]

If you're looking for a unique piece of Kyoto lacquerware, the quality here is a cut above. It all happens in the shadow of the giant vermillion tori gate – the perfect icon to oversee these fine wares. The store stocks a fine line in lacquerware trinkets – everything from chopsticks, striped goblets, soup bowls, sake cups and tea canisters to our favourite, the immaculate apple sugar bowls (pictured at left). Tsunesaburo specialises in lacquerware from two of Japan's most famed areas: **Yamanaka**, which uses the maki-e technique, where gold and silver powders are applied before the lacquer dries; and **Wajima**, which uses the chinkin method of hand-embedding designs onto utensils with gold sheet. If you're into excellent craftsmanship, this is the store for you.

**POCKET TIP**

Head to Kobijutsu-seto next door for the most beautiful selection of ceramics.

## 7. TSUTAYA OKAZAKI

Rohm Theatre, 13 Nijo dori,
Okazaki, Saishojicho,
Sakyo-ku
754 0008
real.tsite.jp/kyoto-okazaki/english/
Mon–Sun 8am–10pm
[MAP 1 F1]

The **Rohm Theatre** has languished by the canal for years but the canny people at Tsutaya took this mid-century brutalist gem and repurposed it into a destination bookstore that has brought young Kyoto back to the area. They hardly touched the building – its temple-shaped roof perfectly reflects the Kyoto monuments in the surrounding hills, and the minimalist grey slate of the exterior is very chic right now. The store is divided into three concepts: 'Japanese Living', 'On Japan' and 'Art', and diverges into local art and handmade crafts. You can lose hours browsing the vast collection, or lounging in the upstairs cafe while flipping lazily through the latest recommendation from Tsutaya's instore concierge. Hire one of their bikes and tour the beautiful north. When you return, grab a magazine or two from their inspirational collection to take back to your room with you.

**POCKET TIP**
Pop into the Ethelvine wine cave and grab some booze for your picnic hamper.

## 8. YOJIYA CAFE

15 Shishigatani, Honenincho,
Sakyo-ku
754 0017
www.yojiya.co.jp/english
Mon–Sun 9.45am–6pm
[MAP 1 G1]

The black-and-white geisha logo of **Yojiya** (*see* p. 90) on the **Philosopher's Path** (*see* p. 104) is a sign that it's time to ponder more immediate needs. After all, even philosophers need a sugar hit every now and then. Follow the sign through the gates and towards the old two-storey machiya (traditional wooden townhouse). Head inside and slip off your shoes, and before you know it you'll be taking tea like it's 1899. Low tables on tatami (straw) mats await lacquerware trays bearing seasonal sweets. Make sure to order the dessert set (at around ¥1000), with a cute hand mirror-shaped wafer, some delicious vanilla ice-cream and fruit or red bean, and a very photographic matcha latte (pictured above) that has a perfectly powdered Yojiya face. You even get a little piece of their famous blotting paper at the end to soak up those pesky facial oils.

# 9. UNITÉ

1F, 133 Shinpontocho,
Sakyo-ku
708 7153
www.unite-kyoto.jp/cafe
Mon–Tues, Thurs–Sun
11.30am–7pm
[MAP 1 E1]

Head down the tiny corridor and give the secret knock. The Showa-era door under the 'Unité' sign will open to reveal a space in two halves. One side is a cafe, where a central table overlooks a quaint garden. You can set up here and order coffee with old-school biscuits or a ¥650 rice ball set. Pick something from the ramshackle bookshelf in the middle to read while sipping iced tea. The second half is a small shop selling beautiful ceramics from famed local makers, and a range of zakka (everyday items), much of which is cat-themed. Yes, they're big on cats here, and you'll find many cat-themed events being touted at the small bar. Settle in and share an intellectual convo or two about music, socialism or cats.

## 10. OMEN

74 Shishigatani dori, Jodoji,
Ishibashicho,
Sakyo-ku
771 8994
omen.co.jp/index.html
Mon–Sun 11am–9pm
[MAP 1 G1]

As you meditate your way along the **Philosopher's Path** (*see* p. 104) you might feel the need to stop and refuel. Omen means 'honourable noodle', and the noodle is revered here in a number of different and delicious ways. Try the Omen Udon – they've named it after themselves, so it has to be good! Fresh, fat, chewy udon noodles are served up with a beautiful array of seasonal vegetables, pickles, toasted sesame seeds and a mountainous pile of daikon (a type of radish). There are great vegan options here, too – many of their soup stocks don't use fish – but for carnivores the duck udon is a standout. Either way, it's a healthy and light meal in a charming, traditional space. Yes, it's popular, and you'll have to queue, but this is one of the best noodle joints in town and it never disappoints.

**POCKET TIP**

Look for the red bird logo to find Chidoriya, a famous Kyoto skin care institution.

## 11. MO-AN

8 Yoshidakaguraokacho,
Sakyo-ku
761 2100
Tues–Sun 11.30am–6pm
[MAP 1 G1]

Ever wanted to be in your own fairytale? You'll have to go deep into the forest to find this tea house in a treehouse, but once the trek is over you'll be rewarded with a magical experience. Dreamily beautiful, this two-storey machiya (traditional wooden townhouse) will quickly put you under its spell. Climb the stairs and take in the woody scent and the dark greens of the trees. Tuck into the matcha affogato, a take on the Italian classic. The magic touch here is that you'll be pouring green tea instead of coffee – eat it quickly before the ice-cream melts into a gooey mess. While away the afternoon with a book, or bring a friend, but remember to speak at a whisper; this is a place of contemplation. Delicious afternoon tea in a quiet woodland retreat – this is enchanted Kyoto at its best.

**POCKET TIP**
Check out Noma, a cool little cafe in the quiet side streets.

# NORTH KYOTO

North Kyoto is having a moment. Kinkakuji, the Golden Pavilion, brings people flocking to this area, but they rarely stay to explore. For those in the know, however, this is the poster precinct for the reinvention of Kyoto, taking ancient traditional beauty and spinning it for the current day. It's a brave new world – Omiya dori is dotted with unique cafes built into beautiful ancient buildings, shops selling contemporary handcrafted items, and eateries where classic Kyoto cuisine is given a new twist. Students are driving the influx of vegetarian cafes, sweet shops and burger joints. The old world still stakes a claim, with markets on the grounds of spectacular temples, antique and vintage stores crammed with oddments and relics, one-of-a-kind Kyoto craft experiences and some long-standing eateries that have perfected many aspects of Kyoto cuisine over time.

SIGHTS
1. Kinkakuji
2. Botanical Gardens
3. Kitano Tenmangu
SHOPPING
4. Nishijin Textile Center
5. Wahindo
6. Kamisoe
7. Squirrel and Sleeping Forest
8. Uchu Wagashi
SHOPPING, EATING AND DRINKING
9. Toraya
10. Stardust
EATING AND DRINKING
11. Seike-Yuba
12. Wife and Husband
13. Sarasa Nishijin
14. Umezono Sabo
平安の郷
こども文庫 きのこの家

## 1. KINKAKUJI

[MAP 3 A3]

A golden pavilion full of whispered stories of a fanatical monk setting it ablaze in 1950 and a Japanese Muromachi strolling garden with bonsai and pines on small islands. What's not to love? The pavilion, clad in gold leaf and gleaming in bright sun or winter light, is heaven for photographers. If you're lucky enough to be there when it's snowing it is truly a sight to behold. You don't have to shave your head to get in – just donate ¥400. In a city with 17 UNESCO World Heritage sights, Kinkakuji still stands out.

## 2. BOTANICAL GARDENS

[MAP 3 C2]

Grab a picnic basket and head to the Botanical Gardens. It's a great escape – people seem to have forgotten it exists, so you may have the iris garden, bonsai exhibits, lotuses, peonies and roses to yourself. Entry is ¥200, and it's worth it for the huge conservatory alone. The children's play area has tall, colourful toadstools, which open up to reveal libraries of vintage children's books. It's also good for cherry blossom viewing: the blossoms hold on just that little bit longer in the enchanted soil.

**POCKET TIP**
Bus 204 goes from Ginkakuji (*see* p. 104) to Kinkakuji.

**KINKAKUJI**
1 Kinkakujicho, Kita-ku
Kitaoji Station or bus no 101, 205
Mon–Sun 9am–5pm

**BOTANICAL GARDENS**
Kitayama dori, Shimogamo Hangicho, Sakyo-ku
Kitayama Station or bus no 205
Mon–Sun 9am–5pm

# 3. KITANO TENMANGU

[MAP 3 A4]

The cherry blossom's oft-overlooked cousin, the ume (plum), is stunning in its own right. Kitano Tenmangu, built in 1607, is one of Kyoto's best viewing spots for the ume blossom. The **Bai-en** garden is in full flower in February. On 25 February geiko and maiko (apprentice geisha) come here to serve matcha and sweets and perform a tea ceremony amid the flowering ume blossoms. Also known for its maple leaves, Kitano Tenmangu's maple garden, **Momiji-en**, is awash with red in autumn. Treasure hunters note, Kitano Tenmangu hosts a fantastic flea market on the 25th of every month, with antiques, vintage textiles, souvenirs and great street food – and it runs from 6am to 9pm! This is also the resting place of Sugawara no Michizane, the first person ever enshrined as a god. He's the god of academics, so say a little prayer and maybe you'll leave just that little bit smarter.

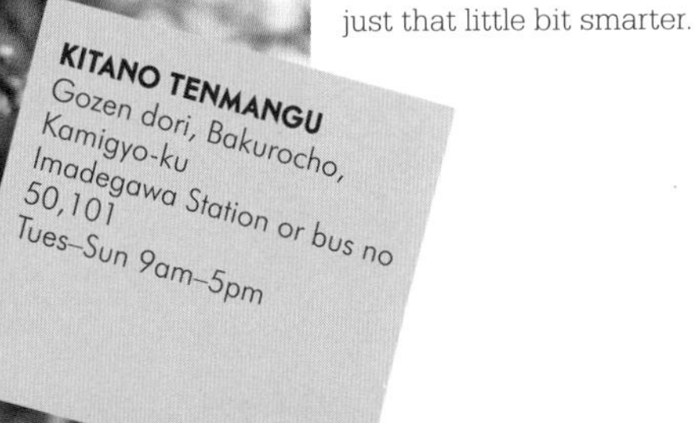

**KITANO TENMANGU**
Gozen dori, Bakurocho, Kamigyo-ku
Imadegawa Station or bus no 50,101
Tues–Sun 9am–5pm

# 4. NISHIJIN TEXTILE CENTER

414 Horikawa dori,
Tatemonzencho,
Kamigyo-ku
451 9231
nishijin.or.jp/eng/brochure
Mon–Sun 10am–6pm
[MAP 3 B5]

The Nishijin Textile Center is resolutely stuck in the '60s, so it's come right back into fashion. A textile showroom with a definite *Mad Men* aesthetic, this mid-century department store is the epitome of retro cool. They present a kimono parade throughout the day, complete with chintzy stage setting and elevator music. Witness Japanese models in full make-up parading in beautiful kimonos to the muzak version of Nirvana's 'Smells Like Teen Spirit'. Upstairs you'll find quality furoshiki (traditional wrapping cloth), tenugui (hand towels), kimonos, obi sashes, silk ties and kokeshi (dolls). Regular weaving demonstrations will bring you up to date on your straight and diagonal interlocking and jacquard patterns. If you want to get hands-on, enrol in a loom weaving class for ¥1800.

**POCKET TIP**
Hire a traditional 12-layered kimono for ¥10,000.

# 5. WAHINDO

190–16 Imadegawa dori,
Nishijozenjicho,
Kamigyo-ku
467 4400
wahindo.jp
Mon–Sun 12–7pm
[MAP 3 A5]

Every oddment and relic in this one-of-a-kind antique store has been chosen because it has a story to tell. Lacquerware, ironwork, old statues – each item is a piece of affordable history that happily wears the marks of time. Wahindo don't care if things are damaged; chips, scratches, scrapes and cracks just add to the beauty. Eclectic ceramics come as sets or one-offs, lonely pieces looking for a home. The owner has a good eye, and you'll need one too – pieces may seem broken or useless, but these pre-loved curios and ephemera trawled up from Kyoto's deep history are a collector's or stylist's dream. The tiny showroom is artfully atmospheric. Warm woods, shoji screens and tatami (straw) mats contrast with bleached branches and strewn pebbles. If you see something you like here, grab it. It's likely to be a singular find.

# 6. KAMISOE

10–1 Kuramaguchi dori,
Murasakino,
Higashifujinomoricho,
Kita-ku
432 8555
http://kamisoe.com
Tues–Sun 12–6pm
[MAP 3 B4]

Ko Kado has been running this shop for three years. He takes his knowledge of graphics to block print onto paper, which he then uses to adorn beautiful shoji screens. In an era of mass production it's refreshing to see someone lovingly crafting traditional objects by hand and adding a contemporary twist. New makers are moving into the area and blending traditional craftsmanship with modern design. But you don't have to be in need of a shoji screen. One of the great things about Kamisoe is that shoji paper is also used for stationery. The exquisite paper is repurposed into notepads and envelopes with the quality of times gone by.

## 7. SQUIRREL AND SLEEPING FOREST

74 Tenji dori, Nishimachi, Kamigyo-ku
467 2120
kyoto.zaq.ne.jp/squirrel
www3.to/sleeping-forest
Fri–Sat 12–5pm
[MAP 3 A5]

If you've ever wanted to follow Alice down the rabbit hole, you've come to the right place. Owner Mika Takeo, aka Ri_bon, is an antique collector, artist and renowned local maker of handcrafted accessories who has a thing for doilies, music boxes, toadstools and vintage playing cards. You'll find her fairytale-themed creations in the Sleeping Forest – climb the narrow stairs to a secret attic decorated with Alice in Wonderland silhouettes and fairy lights. A table sprouts moss and displays small key and mushroom brooches, rosettes, buttons and cookies, all illustrated with Ri_bon's take on English fables and nostalgia. Ground-level Squirrel is an antiques store populated by Ri_bon's superb collection of European whimsy and nostalgic ephemera. Rifling through old letters and postcards is bound to put you in a sentimental state of mind. Make sure you visit on weekends – the Squirrel and the Forest like to sleep during the week.

## 8. UCHU WAGASHI

786 Fujikicho,
Kamigyo-ku
201 4933
http://uchu-wagashi.jp
Tues–Sun 10am–6pm
[MAP 3 B4]

Uchu is unique. We can't think of another place on Earth that makes modernist candy. Experimental, evolutionary North Kyoto is the perfect place for a streamlined, minimalist store specialising in rakugan, wasanbon and konpeito, hard candy made from sugar rice flower. The shapes and designs are new to Japan, and will surprise and delight any rock candy fan. The 'drawing candy' for ¥650 is great fun – graphic shapes that can be rearranged into objects and animals. Boxes packed with small konpeito candy are also ¥650 and feature tiny clouds, fish, birds, aeroplanes, houses and hot-air balloons. The animal set comes complete with cute hedgehog. It's adorable, packaged beautifully and will appeal equally to both adults and children. The box will be on display on your shelf for ages before you realise it's probably time to eat its contents.

# 9. TORAYA

Karasuma dori, Ichijokado,
Kamigyo-ku
441 3111
www.toraya-group.co.jp/english
Mon–Sun 9am–7pm
[MAP 3 C5]

Toraya have been making exquisite wagashi (sweets) since the 1500s. Now in their 17th generation, this amazing family have upheld the principles of reflecting nature and the seasons in their beautiful creations made from 'An', the red bean. Toraya wish to engage the five senses. Just seeing these incredible sweets will make you want to touch, taste and smell them – and then you'll hear the sounds of joy they evoke in people. Toraya's purity and simplicity mean it looks as fresh today as it did 500 years ago. This tearoom is the new face of Toraya, contemporary and architecturally designed, with an arched wooden roof, water features, a relaxing outdoor zone overlooking Japanese gardens and tori gates, and an adjoining gallery showing beautifully curated exhibitions. It's where art and sweets meet. You may want to frame the packaging – it's elegantly designed and iconic.

## 10. STARDUST

41 Shichiku, Shimotakedonocho, Kita-ku
286 7296
http://stardustkyoto.com
Tues–Sun 11am–6pm, closed Mon first Sat & Sun of every month
[MAP 3 B2]

Time moves differently at Stardust. The space is part cafe and part 'beautiful things'. Book in advance for the cafe; their seasonal vegan lunch is made in limited quantities. Pair it with an organic wine or whimsically presented seasonal fruit juice, which comes in Osaka's Ricordo glassware, and follow with one of their delicious 'raw sweets', presented on exquisite crockery like tiny pieces of art with little wisps of nature. Flora and fauna displays, brass crystals and candle holders adorn mismatched wooden tables. Host Kana floats in and out of the rooms, radiating universal energy. Nature floats in and out of the rustic space as well – balls of moss form on concrete, and tendrils of greenery weave in and out of the room. The 'beautiful things' come in the form of artfully curated ceramics, textiles and jewellery and the wafting elegance of Cosmic Wonder's designer clothing. Books, coffee beans and more are all chosen because they light up their own little corner of the universe.

POCKET TIP
Great coffee can be found at nearby Circus Coffee and Cafe 1001.

## 11. SEIKE-YUBA

234 Omiya dori, Yakushicho, Kamigyo-ku
468 8487
http://seike-yuba.com
Mon–Sun (lunch) 11.30am–2.30pm, Mon–Tues 5–9pm, closed Wed
[MAP 3 B5]

While escaping Christmas in Kyoto, we ambled through the northern streets looking for somewhere to have a special lunch. We came across the elegant exterior of an old townhouse with white noren (traditional fabric) flags emblazoned with pink sakura (cherry blossoms). It was a yuba specialist (yuba is the skin that forms on the top of tofu). The setting was exquisite, the food was vegetarian, the price was amazing – a Christmas miracle! To this day it's one of our fondest memories. The 11-course meal featured soup, sashimi yuba, a bubbling yuba hot pot with mountain vegetables and soy milk pudding – there were so many delicious variations on this soft-textured, rough-edged delicacy. The room is an elegant piece of history, with low-hanging lanterns, shoji screens, hallways disappearing to parts unknown, and wood-framed windows overlooking tranquil gardens. At ¥4100–¥5900 you'll be living a shogun's lifestyle on a peasant's budget.

## 12. WIFE AND HUSBAND

106–6, Koyamashimouchi-kawaracho,
Kita-ku
201 7324
wifeandhusband.jp
Tues, Wed & Fri 10am–5pm, check online calendar for opening days and times
[MAP 3 C3]

The owners of Wife and Husband say that they roasted coffee beans on the first day they spent together, and they've done it every day since. They want to connect with us 'the way the word husband connects with wife', words that cannot exist except in combination. Hang around the back streets if you have to wait for a table, then head inside for pour-over coffee at ¥550–¥600 or some of their delectable honey cheese toast. Antiques, found furniture, hanging dried flowers, broken clocks and hanging bicycles warm up the space. Take away Wife and Husband's appropriately named 'Daughter' blend coffee for ¥1200, or on a nice day, head here for picnic supplies. They sell hampers and you can rent a stool, a straw hat, a parasol and a folding table for anywhere between ¥150 and ¥400. With the **Botanical Gardens** (*see* p. 116) and the river nearby, who can resist?

## 13. SARASA NISHIJIN

11–1 Kuramaguchi dori,
Murasakino,
Higashifujinomoricho,
Kita-ku
432 5075
http://sarasan2.exblog.jp
Mon–Sun 12–11pm
[MAP 3 B4]

Sarasa Nishijin was once a sento (public bathhouse), where people came to relax and soak away their cares. Now converted into a fantastic cafe, you can still come here to relax, but it's probably best to keep your clothes on. Pause outside and take in the amazing frontage. This is one of the finest examples of the beautiful old buildings being repurposed and contemporised in North Kyoto. That majestic roof, the original tiles slightly obscured by rows of bicycles – it's picturesque. The tiles continue inside, covering the walls and giving the space an almost Moroccan look. Original walls partition the room, and noren (traditional fabric) flags hint at what has gone before. It's spacious for a Kyoto cafe, so make yourself at home and order up an omelette, a pizza, or a **Clamp coffee** (*see* p. 140). Those who loved the bathhouse might lament its loss, but cafe fans have a new go-to.

**POCKET TIP**
Soak away the afternoon at iconic Funaoka Onsen, one of Kyoto's old-school local bathhouses.

## 14. UMEZONO SABO

11–1 Kuramaguchi dori,
Murasakino,
Higashifujinomoricho,
Kita-ku
432 5088
http://umezono-kyoto.com
Mon–Sun 11am–6.30pm
[MAP 3 B4]

An unassuming entryway with a tiny bonsai and a blackboard with minimal kanji hides a truly beautiful North Kyoto experience. This is a sweet store operating on another plane. Inside, the downstairs counter sells ten different species of delectable wagashi (sweets), perched on tiny white pedestals like works of art. For the premium experience, climb the steep stairs and head into a room of brushed walls, exposed original beams and warm wood furniture. This is the immaculate setting for perfectly blended tea, whisked matcha or homemade fruit drink and some of the finest cakes we've ever had. The Japanese think there's a European element to the sweets, but the wormwood with bean jam, white bean with almonds and mugwort soy flour with almonds, all topped with lemon cream and roasted tea icing, are uniquely Japanese. It's a contemporary, chic wagashi update and a perfect example of the city's inventive north.

# NIJO

Presided over by ancient and proud Nijo Castle, one of Kyoto's most popular attractions, Nijo is an area of stark contrasts. Open boulevards and residential blocks are punctuated by laneways that hide cool new additions to Kyoto's retail and eating experiences. This is a place for walking and discovering. Wherever you go, the expansive castle grounds will be in sight – the high walls offering tantalising glimpses of what lies beyond. You can only enter the castle grounds from the east. As you do, you can admire the white towers peeking over the grey walls and the wide moat that defends the castle from attack, although the only assault these days comes from busloads of tourists.

You're in ninja territory now, so slide down side streets and sneak into buildings to uncover contemporary Nijo. Sidle into antique stores to unearth some gems from Kyoto's distant past. Pad quietly into old townhouses that have been turned into very special cafe experiences, or blend silently into contemporary coffee shops and eateries that put a new spin on the traditional.

**SIGHTS**

1. Nijo Castle
2. Kyoto International Manga Museum

**SHOPPING**

3. The Kyoto Shibori Museum
4. Banbutsusozobo
5. Cotoha

**SHOPPING AND EATING**

6. Songbird
7. Iyemon Salon

**EATING AND DRINKING**

8. Clamp Coffee Sarasa
9. Kotobanohaoto

# 1. NIJO CASTLE

[MAP 3 B7]

Built in 1603, Nijo Castle was the residence of the first Edo era shogun Tokugawa Iyeyasu. Shoguns, ninja warriors, the drama of battle – Nijo's history as a feudal site has made it one of the most visited places in Kyoto. Assault the castle from the east gate. The first defence is the ticket machine, but quick use should secure you permission to enter. Once inside, pass unchallenged through the ornate **Karamon Gate** and head into the **Ninomaru Palace**, where the shogun stayed when he visited Kyoto. The detailed carving on the gate and the striking wooden roof show an astounding level of craftsmanship. Inside the palace, the rooms are connected by the fun 'nightingale floors', which squeak when stepped on, an ancient version of the security alarm. Elsewhere you'll find the ruins of the old keep, and the **Ninomaru Garden** – the very definition of a Japanese ornamental garden, its pond surrounded by pine trees. The castle is made up of three circles of defence. Breach all three and award yourself a ninja gold star.

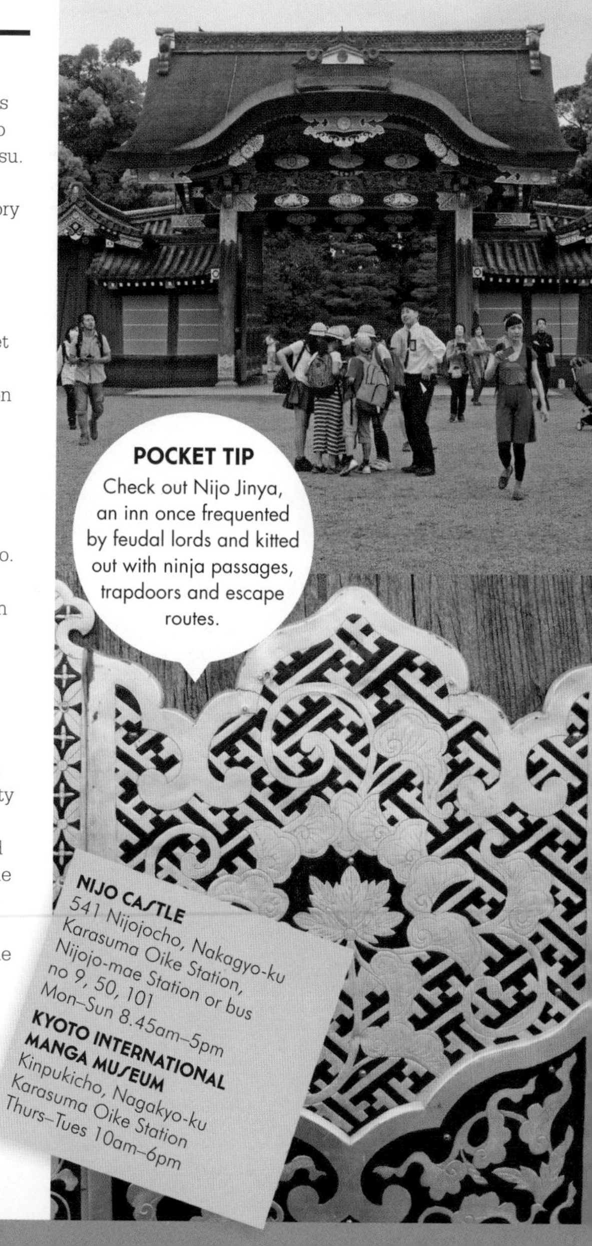

**POCKET TIP**

Check out Nijo Jinya, an inn once frequented by feudal lords and kitted out with ninja passages, trapdoors and escape routes.

**NIJO CASTLE**
541 Nijojocho, Nakagyo-ku
Karasuma Oike Station, Nijojo-mae Station or bus no 9, 50, 101
Mon–Sun 8.45am–5pm

**KYOTO INTERNATIONAL MANGA MUSEUM**
Kinpukicho, Nagakyo-ku
Karasuma Oike Station
Thurs–Tues 10am–6pm

## 2. KYOTO INTERNATIONAL MANGA MUSEUM

[MAP 1 B2]

Do you have a deep and abiding love for Astroboy? Are you crazy for '60s illustrations? The 300,000 items on display at the Kyoto International Manga Museum are bound to please. Museum makes it sound like a grey hall of static exhibits, but in this space, the phrase 'do not touch' doesn't apply. Bookshelves stretch from floor to ceiling, and you can pluck out any comic at will and start reading. It's a celebration of the form, a place where manga fans and comic art obsessives can admire the technical skill and sheer crazy beauty of the flat, bold colours and eye-popping graphics. Permanent exhibitions include the popular maiko (apprentice geisha) illustrations and a 'What is manga?' exposé. You can join special classes and learn how to 'build' your own manga character. Regular sessions of Kamishibai, the traditional form of storytelling with pictures, show how deep the roots of manga go. Even in this most Japanese of places, there's an 'only in Japan' moment – check out the display of plaster casts of the hands of visiting manga artists.

## 3. THE KYOTO SHIBORI MUSEUM

Shikiamicho, Aburanokouji, Nakagyo-ku
221 4252
http://kyotoshiborimuseum.wix.com/kyoto-shibori-museum
Mon–Sun 9am–5pm
[MAP 1 A2]

The art of shibori (dyeing fabric) is one of the most refined aspects of Japanese culture. Shibori are mostly brought to life using indigo dye, which produces exquisite patterns on silk, hemp and cotton by using knotting, pleating and stitching techniques that bind the cloth. This technique has a 1300-year history, celebrated in this museum, which is a must-see for textile and craft enthusiasts. Exhibits take you through the history of shibori and showcase many fine examples. There's plenty of educational fun to be had too. Learn to make your own shibori, dyeing and wrapping cloth, and fumbling your way through the various binding methods. Entry to the museum is ¥500, but you can pay ¥3000 for the 60-minute class or ¥5000 for the masterclass, both of which can be conducted in English. The museum shop has shibori products and accessories, and they even have a fun kimono fitting service.

**POCKET TIP**
Try on a kimono in the museum shop – they will gladly take photos for you!

# 4. BANBUTSUSOZOBO

60–1 Horikawa dori,
Sanbohorikawacho,
Nakagyo-ku
256 0552
http://homepage3.nifty.com/NEMURENUYORU/banbutsu
Mon–Sun 2–7pm
[MAP 3 B7]

The ramshackle frontage, nearly obscured by pot plants, curiosities, statues and samurai swords, says it all – this is a scavenger's dream. It's hard to tell where the owner's collection ends and the shop begins. Inside the tiny space Nintendo console games and Buddha statuettes sit happily side by side. If you're into '70s kung-fu movies but also have a secret love for antique ceramics, you've come to the right place. Add to your Japanese doll collection while surreptitiously grabbing some banned '70s flicks on video. Retro children's books, Miffy and Hello Kitty battle for shelf space with china teapots and Japanese musical instruments. The walls are plastered with retro advertising, taxidermy, weird clocks and Japanese 45s. So make like Bruce Lee and manoeuvre yourself deftly towards a cash register covered in tiny toys. This anarchic jumble of pop culture and traditional Kyoto antiques will be unlike anything you've seen.

# 5. COTOHA

67–38 Nishinokyo, Shokushicho, Nakagyo-ku
802 9108
cotoha.me
Mon–Sun 11am–6pm
[MAP 3 A7]

The use of nature in homes is probably the biggest trend in interior design right now. Kyoto's deep understanding of the natural world puts it at the forefront of this trend, and Cotoha take it a step further with their extraordinary warehouse jungle. Climb the stairs, being careful not to get entangled in the vines and tendrils of verdant vegetation that weave and curl around banisters and balustrades. This is wild nature let loose – a Japanese Day of the Triffids with floor-to-ceiling and wall-to-wall greenery. The beautiful and eclectic array of plants, accessories, vintage plant pots, industria and racks or repurposed indoor garden antiques showcase a store that utilises some of Earth's oldest living things to enhance some of the most contemporary spaces. Downstairs, the florist **Blowmist Boom** is the perfect place to grab a bouquet for your new best friend or Airbnb host.

**POCKET TIP**
The beautiful Shinsenen gardens are worth a visit on the way to Clamp and Cotoha.

## 6. SONGBIRD

529 Nishitakeyacho,
Nakagyo-ku
221 0351
songbird-design.jp/store.html
Tues–Sun 12–8pm, closed Thurs
[MAP 3 B6]

Modern Kyoto is multitasking, and Songbird, where coffee meets design meets workspace meets gallery, is leading the pack. Even the building, circa 1904, makes an interesting counterpoint to the centuries-old townhouses being turned into cafes all over the city. Songbird is an arts and design hub for the self-employed and a drop-in centre where they welcome everyone from businessmen to students to breastfeeding mothers or LGBTQ. You might see hip kids designing on their laptops, or new mothers enjoying the banana cheese terrine or a butterscotch strawberry pineapple tea. Coffee is taken seriously here. Lattes and cappuccinos are single origin pour-over, and cold brew coffee is steeped for 24 hours. If your cold-brew isn't cold enough you can give it the nitrogen treatment, or try the espresso spritzer – sparkling water, ice and agave add a unique twist to your everyday pick-me-up. As they say at Songbird, they're 'an extension of your living room'. Pop in – you'll feel right at home.

## 7. IYEMON SALON

80 Sanjo dori, Mikuracho, Nakagyo-ku
222 1500
http://iyemonsalon.jp
Mon–Sun 8am–11.30pm
[MAP 1 B3]

Early riser? Late sleeper? Iyemon Salon has you covered. It's open from 8am until last drinks, with free wi-fi and delicious breakfast, lunch and dinner sets. You could park yourself here and stay all day. Settle in on a Scandi swan chair or take a seat on the decking overlooking the rambling Japanese garden and tuck into pork and egg sandwiches, washed down with a naughty-but-nice morning cocktail of yoghurt, berry and tea with a splash of booze. For something outside the box, try the green tea beer. Lunch and dinner sets are feasts, but locals flock here for oyatsu (afternoon tea). The tasting set of nine delectable treats goes perfectly with a midori green tea, honey chai or one of the delicious tea cocktails. Browse or spend up at their mini floor-level shop, or head upstairs for a more comprehensive look at new Kyoto designer versions of tea accessories, ceramics and beautifully packaged boxes of their own tea.

**POCKET TIP**

Book into nearby Ramen University and learn the way of the noodle.

## 8. CLAMP COFFEE SARASA

67–38 Nishinokyo, Shokushicho, Nakagyo-ku
822 9397
sp.raqmo.com/cafe-sarasa
Mon–Sun 11am–6pm
[MAP 3 A7]

Some people come to this area to visit **Nijo Castle** (*see* p. 132). Coffee pilgrims head straight to Clamp Coffee Sarasa. A clamp grips the counter with a sign above it that says 'cramp coffee', no doubt a wry in-joke, but coffee here is a serious business. Walls and shelves are cluttered with mismatched Americana (the United States flag greets you as you enter), but don't expect a caramel latte or frappuccino. Coffee here is pour-over, single origin, and they take their time getting it right. The cafe only seats about 12, with most of the space in the room taken up by a huge (functioning) coffee bean roaster. They sell bags of their expertly roasted beans, so you can take some Clamp home with you. Join the communal table or take a chair by the window and sip excellent coffee to a soundtrack of American country and blues. The wall says it all: 'One of the great joys in life is coffee and good conversation'.

ONE OF THE
GREAT JOYS
IN LIFE IS
COFFEE AND
GOOD
CONVERSATION
Social walk
OFF SEASON

# 9. KOTOBANOHAOTO

34 Aburanokoji dori,
Daikokuyacho,
Kamigyo-ku
414 2050
kotobanohaoto.net/contents
Wed–Sun 11.30am–7.30pm
[MAP 3 B6]

Only in Japan will you find a cat-themed dessert house, and only in Kyoto will you find it in a beautiful old machiya (traditional wooden townhouse). Follow the cat on the noren (traditional fabric) curtains as he beckons you inside. Take a seat – you might be waiting a while, but this is an experience you simply cannot find anywhere else. Soon you'll be ushered into a quiet room with cute couples on dates and friends catching up over a matcha latte. There's plenty of cattitude in the room. Cheeky cat ceramics and maneki-neko (lucky cat) figurines pop out of bookcases, vintage books and games fill the shelves and quiet music drifts from an '80s sound system. You can draw your own cats in the books provided, but it's all passing time while you wait for your dessert, the super-cute Cat Parfait (pictured at far right), an ice-cream cat head bobbing out of a sundae glass crammed with biscuits and jelly. In a country of cute, this is a high point.

# ARASHIYAMA

Arashiyama has it all – mountains, forests, rivers, secret shrines and great shopping and eating.

The Togetsu 'Moon Crossing' Bridge has great mountain views with autumnal foliage, cherry blossoms or blankets of snow, depending on the season. It's all about the bamboo grove, though, so detour upriver and you'll soon be strolling through a forest thick with towering bamboo trees. There are endless photo opportunities here, but they won't do justice to the deep smell of wood and dirt, and the wonderful stillness. If the kids are getting restless, take them up to Iwatayama Monkey Park, where they can watch hundreds of the little scamps swinging from trees, grooming each other and casting disdainful looks in your general direction.

Head to Okochi Sanso, the former home of silent-film star Denjiro Okochi, where you can explore the gardens and enjoy the stunning views for free. Then for a real taste of old Kyoto, head to Saga Torimoto, a preserved street from the Meiji era. If you're doing the World Heritage tour visit Rinzai Buddhist temple Tenryu-ji. The garden has been designated a 'Special Place of Scenic Beauty of Japan'. Otagi Nen-Butsu-ji features 1200 moss-covered statues of Rakan, Buddha's disciples.

At Randen Saga Station you'll find the popular Kimono Forest – 600 poles covered with 32 differently patterned fabrics. Your tired feet will love you if you head to Onsen Ekino Ashiyu, where for ¥200 you can soak them in the hot springs footbath within the station.

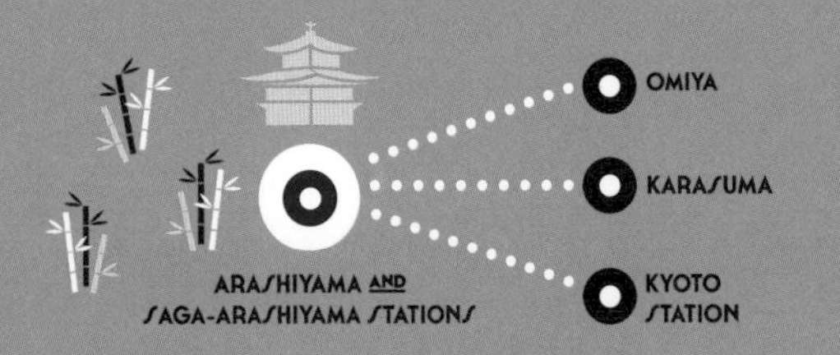

## ARASHIYAMA SHOPPING AND EATING

Food and retail choices are plentiful in Arashiyama. Vegetarians will want to head to **Macrobiotics Prunus**, across the road from Saga Arashiyama Station's south gate. Vegetarians and tofu lovers will want to try the 'yudo' at **Yadofu Sagano** – simmered chunks of tofu with various side dishes. Converted public bathhouse **Sagano-Yu** has coffee and cafe-style meals with a focus on pastas and curries. Their green tea and black syrup parfait is perfect on hot days. If you want the perfect Tofu Kaiseki, head to **Shoraian**, on the edge of a mountain overlooking the Oi River. Three sets are priced at ¥38, ¥46, ¥58 – a great way to have excellent Kaiseki without the premium price tag. The Arashiyama branch of the **Yoshimura soba** group is their most picturesque, so head here if you're a fan of perfect buckwheat noodles. Food and drink are everywhere, but the excellent range of sweet shops here is worth a special mention. There are plenty of craft and homewares stores to visit, too. **Chirimen Zaikukan** is a craft museum showcasing the colourful history of handmade Kyoto. You can buy small imperial dolls, purses, hairclips, toys and fabrics. **Platz** has an extensive range of homewares and Japanese souvenirs.

# THE EIZAN LINE

The Eizan Electric Railway is basically the train set you had as a kid, but all grown up. There's something relaxing and old-world about riding this line as it winds its way into the northern mountains. Many of the stations are small and only manned by one attendant. The trains are colourful, compact and cute, and often only have one carriage. For extra atmosphere, ride the super-cute red D0900, nicknamed Kirara, with the maple leaf on the front. He's the little red carriage that could. As the train climbs further into the mountains and the scenery moves from urban to forest, you'll start to feel like you've left civilisation behind. It's especially stunning in autumn when the train passes through 'the maple leaf tunnel'. Why not have breakfast in Demachiyanagi, followed by an onsen (hot spring) in Kurama and lunch in Kibune, then stop off in Ichijoji for ramen and finish the day in one of Demachiyanagi's bars? Heaven.

The Eizan Line's three platforms can be found on a small retro station within Demachiyanagi. A ride on the Eizan Line will cost you around ¥420 for a 30-minute journey. If you are heading to Kibune or Kurama, make sure you take the correct line – you want the Eizan Kurama Line. The main Eizan Line separates at Takaragaike Station and goes to the base of Mount Hiei.

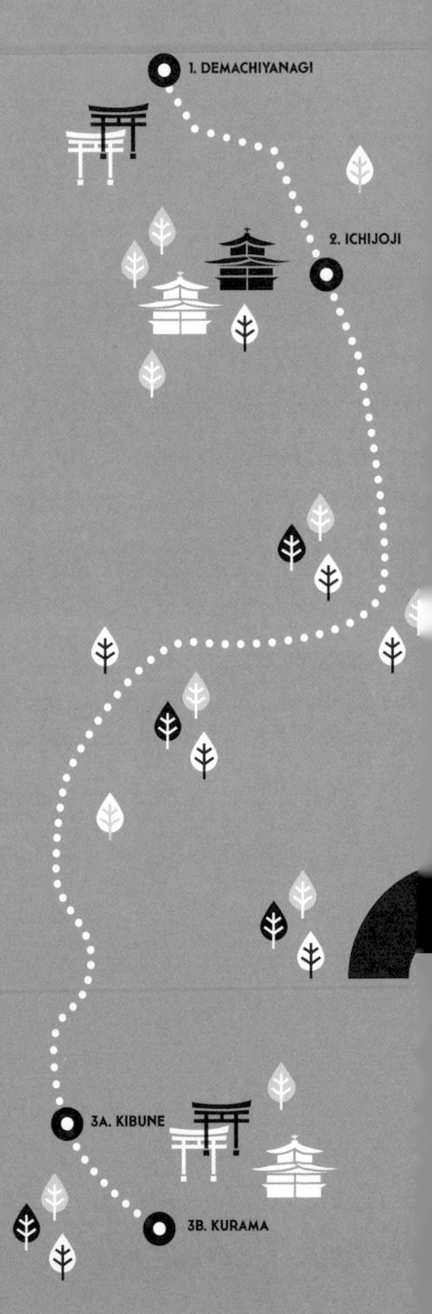

出町柳
ワンマン
EIDEN
902
2

1.

DEMACHIYANAGI

## DEMACHIYANAGI ATTRACTIONS

Demachiyanagi is a breezy university town with plenty of students tucking into vegetarian eats and good coffee. It's local Kyoto going about its day, swapping ideas and sharing philosophies. Cute new indie cafes sit happily alongside eateries and hole-in-the-wall food stops that have been there for over a hundred years. Demachiyanagi sits on the **Kamogawa Delta**, the point where the Kamo River gets into its own heated philosophical debate, splits into two schools of thought and heads into the mountains. Try your luck crossing the river on the famed stepping stones – the mismatched shapes, turtles and birds provide a fun challenge. Demachiyanagi is a great place to grab coffee or breakfast in the morning, or to hit a burger or falafel joint or a bar at night, making it the perfect base camp for a day on the Eizan Line. If you're exploring the shrines and temples of Kyoto, you won't want to miss **Shimogamo**. A sanctuary within a deep green forest on the Kamagawa Delta, this is the oldest Shinto shrine in Kyoto, dating back to the sixth century. Vermillion gates and bridges, moss-covered trees and secret tiny shrines make this a magical escape from the outside world.

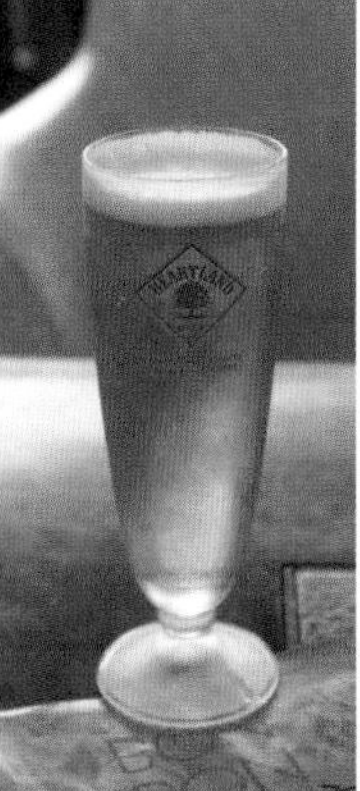

## DEMACHIYANAGI SHOPPING AND EATING

Start the day with breakfast at old-school **Cafe Maki**. Its cute retro signage and so-unstylish-it's-cool interior still have faint echoes of intellectuals' conversations from the '60s. Grab a coffee – they roast it on the premises – a salad and an artfully arranged meat sandwich. Then why not join the long line at **Futaba** and score some of their famous mame-mochi (black bean in soft rice cakes)? If you want to sip coffee or have a late night drink while gazing at the river, **Cafe Bon Bon** is right on the bridge, and the cheery side room overlooks the Delta and the famous stepping stones. **Cafe S.O.U. Violet and Claire** is a tiny bar and cafe with a small gallery. They sell T-shirts, vinyl, zines and indie merch, and host music nights and exhibitions of local handmade craft. Stroll around – there are plenty of vintage and zakka (everyday items) stores to explore. If you're here for lunch or later in the day, join the students and locals at the popular vegan **Felafel Garden** or head to **Salutya**, a cafe housed in an old machiya (traditional wooden townhouse) that does Western-style burgers as well as coffee, beer and a black sesame potato salad that you'll still be thinking about long after you've left.

## 2. ICHIJOJI

## ICHIJOJI ATTRACTIONS

Only three stops from Demachiyanagi, Ichijoji is fast getting a reputation as the new northern soul. It's neighbourhood Kyoto at its finest – amiable, slightly dishevelled, and a magnet for the coolest Kyoto kids. Jump off the Eizan Line and explore. Turn right from the train for ramen and shopping. Turn left and you'll be at the foothills of the mountains. **Shisen-do** and **Enko-ji** are Buddhist temples made all the more beautiful by the mountain atmosphere. If you have the stamina, we recommend hiking all the way to **Tanukidani Fudoin,** the raccoon dog temple, a wooden structure with coloured flags and an amazing view. Raccoon dog statues are everywhere – pray to them for everything from becoming a better driver to preventing cancer. With beautiful mountain walks a stone's throw away and some of the best ramen, coffee and craft beer you'll find, you can bet Ichijoji won't remain a Kyoto secret for long.

## ICHIJOJI SHOPPING AND EATING

Bibliophiles make the trek to Ichijoji for **Keibunsha**, a chic bookstore that often pops up in 'best in the world' lists. The artfully curated selection of books, stationery, and art is described in reverent tones on blogs and in insider magazines. The minimalist lines and contemporary design add to the attraction – in its way, this is a modern shrine to design, art and theory, with a few children's books thrown in for good measure. Along the strip there are plenty of zakka (everday items) stores to explore. If you need a coffee hit, head to **Akatsuki**. This streamlined cafe at the end of Higashi Oji dori does an excellent brew. If you find yourself getting hungry, you just happen to be in ramen heaven. Chicken broth is a big specialty; try **Chinyuu**, **Yuhi no Kirameki**, **Menya Gokkei** or **Tentenyuu**, all of which specialise in the chicken style. If you prefer a more traditional pork broth, head to **Butanchu**, but there are so many choices here for the ramen lover, you really can't go wrong. There are plenty of bars on the strip as well. Cap your day off with a tipple or two at **Tingara** brewpub. Run by Ichijoji's brewery, this cosy little drop-in specialises in fruit beer and is the perfect way to round off your Ichijoji day trip.

## KIBUNE AND KURAMA ATTRACTIONS

For a magical daytrip deep in the northern hills of Kyoto, you can't beat Kibune and Kurama. The two stops at the end of the Eizan Line are all about forest walks, onsens (hot springs), fresh mountain air and small towns with plenty of old-world charm. Kurama's quaint station is overlooked by the head of a prodigiously nosed **Tengu Spirit King**. Catch the shuttle to **Kurama Onsen**, where you can soak your cares away in the hot spring water while taking in a view that's equally beautiful in the winter snow or summer greenery. It's also a ryokan (inn), so if you want to stay longer in the mountain air, book in for the night. You can hike across to Kibune from here (and vice versa), stopping along the way at **Kuramadera Temple**. Climb the steps to the temple, or get on the funicular railway at Sanmon Station and take the easy way up. This temple of the Tendai sect is unique in that it worships an esoteric being called Sonten. Hiking across the mountains is especially spectacular in sakura (cherry blossom) season or during autumn. But if you don't feel like making the trek, catch the shuttle back to Kurama Station and go one stop back to Kibune.

## KIBUNE SHOPPING AND EATING

The walk from Kibune Station into town takes around 45 minutes and is framed by forests, mountain streams, waterfalls and rocky outcrops. The light filtering through the tall trees is enchanting, especially when you reach peaceful **Kibune Shrine**, with its tori gates, vermillion lanterns and steep stairs. In the picturesque town of Kibune you'll find shops selling trinkets and souvenirs, soft-serve ice-cream vendors and the charming **Kibune Onsen** with its moss-covered water wheel. When it comes to food, trekkers will find themselves with an abundance of delicious lunchtime choices for all budgets. When the heat starts to set in, restaurants along the river set up platforms across the water. Drinking in the fresh mountain air, the sound of the water flowing beneath you or rushing over waterfalls, and the lanterns hanging over the platforms make for a very romantic experience. There are plenty of eateries specialising in different types of food, and each has a different riverscape or type of lantern. Make sure to check out **Hirobun**. The Kaiseki lunch is around ¥4000, which includes the fun Nagashi Somen, where soba noodles slide down bamboo pipes and you have to gather them up with your chopsticks.

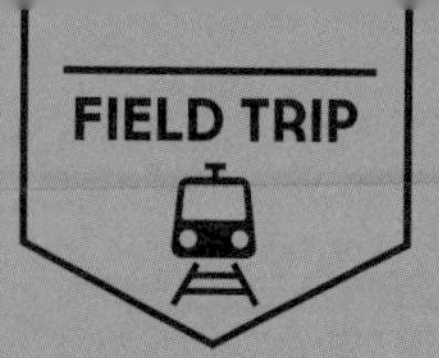


# THE NARA LINE

You'll want to make good use of the Nara Line. The main destinations along it hold the key to some of Kyoto's best sights and daytrips. Jump on and off and explore the wonders of Tofukuji, Inari and Uji, as well as the popular Nara. Pack a bento (takeout) or plan a food stop, and bring a picnic in spring and summer. Why not soak away an afternoon in an onsen (hot spring) – try Hourai Onsen in Nara – or book a ryokan (inn) and stay overnight in Uji or Nara. It's possible to do all four stops in one day, but our advice is: don't rush it. Take the time to really explore – each place could easily fill a day in itself. If you only have one day, try this grab bag of cultural delights: start your day at Tofukuji (it opens at 8.30am), then head to Uji for a green tea noodle lunch and a matcha soft serve, and pop in to spectacular Byodoin for an unforgettable history and cultural lesson. Then head to Nara for an afternoon of temples, deer petting, walks and shopping for handcrafts. On the way home, drop in at Inari to enjoy the beauty of the shrine at dusk and round out the day with a temple street food dinner.

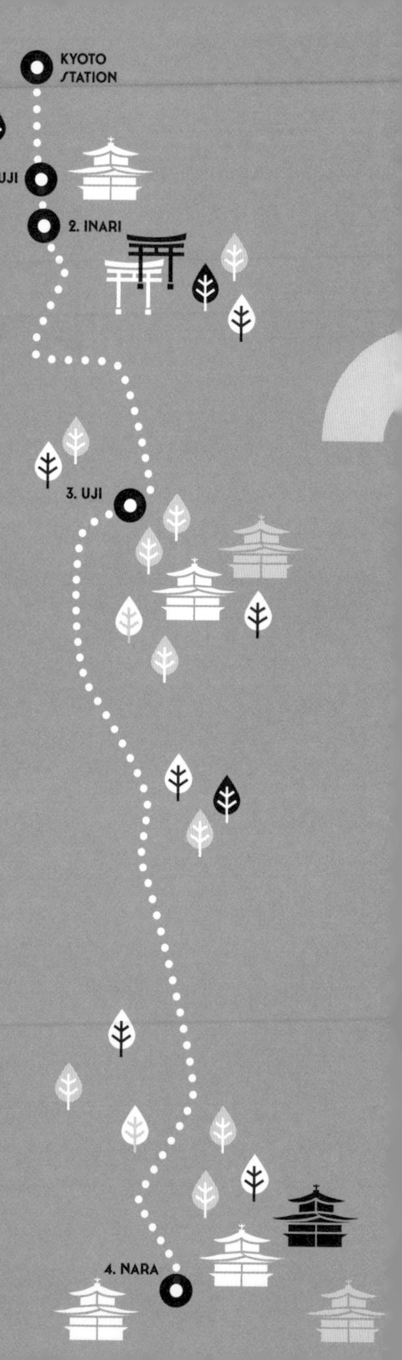

**POCKET TIP**

The Nara Line leaves Kyoto Station from platforms 8, 9 and 10.

# 1. TOFUKUJI

## TOFUKUJI

Tofukuji is a three-minute ride from Kyoto Station on the Nara Line. From there, it's a pleasant ten-minute walk through neighbourhood Kyoto to a tranquil Zen temple complex that is particularly resplendent in autumn. The first thing you'll see is a covered wooden bridge in the distance. Cross this to get to the temple grounds. Built in 1236 to rival Nara, Tofukuji was faithfully reconstructed in the 15th century and stands as a great example of a medieval Zen temple. The **Sanmon** gate is the oldest Zen temple gate in Japan. Although the hondo (main hall) is a more recent structure, the zendo (meditating hall), yokushitsu (bathing room) and the tosu (a large, communal 14th-century outdoor lavatory) are the original buildings. No Zen temple would be complete without a Zen garden, and Tofukuji has four. The 'southern' garden at the hojo, or head priest's quarters, is the most revered. The raked garden's moss and rocks are positioned to reflect the positions of important Zen temples and islands around the world. Of the three spectacular covered wooden bridges, the **Tsutenko** (bridge to heaven) is the prime spot for a view celebrating the full autumnal colours.

**POCKET TIP**

Tofukuji is a residential area, so head to Inari or stay in Kyoto for lunch or dinner.

## 2. INARI

## FUSHIMI INARI SHRINE

Inari Station is around 15 minutes from Kyoto Station on the JR Nara Line (don't take the rapid, it doesn't stop at Inari), or you can take the Keihan Line to Fushimi Inari Station. Inari, the spirit fox, is one of the principal spirits of the Shinto sect. In charge of tea, rice, sake, agriculture, fertility and commerce, Inari clearly has a lot to do, and the fox has around 32,000 dedicated shrines dotted around Japan. Fushimi Inari is the head shrine, a proud vermillion structure with tori gates and fox statues around the grounds. For a once-in-a-lifetime experience, hike up **Inari Mountain**. A tunnel of tori gates, each donated by a business, trails up the mountains for 4 kilometres (2.5 miles). Smaller Inari shrines pop up along the way, as well as a few tea houses where you can stop for tea or perhaps a hot sake. It's a popular destination – early morning or the fading light of dusk are the best times to visit, but you can escape the crowds by making the entire two-hour trek up the mountain.

## INARI SHOPPING AND EATING

En route to the Fushimi Inari Shrine from Fushimi Inari Station you'll find many street stalls and shops selling trinkets such as small tori gates, fox figurines and assorted Inari icons. There's plenty of street food, too. Brightly coloured stalls line the streets leading to the shrine, selling a variety of tasty hand-held food. **Kyozuan** has many varieties of tofu soft serve (pictured below) – try one, it's addictive. There's plenty of yakitori (grilled meat) in the area, the favourite being a splayed sparrow, skewered and char-grilled, but if your taste doesn't extend to tiny birds there's a wide range of beef, chicken and vegetables. For those with a sweet tooth, dango (pictured above) are also in abundance. Don't forget to try some of the Fushimi Inari Shrine's namesake sushi, delicious sweetened rice wrapped in yuba (tofu skin) sheets. Finish off with some tsujiura senbei, a Japanese version of the fortune cookie that dates back to the 19th century.

**POCKET TIP**
Visit Harushika brewery for a sake tour and tasting.

## UJI ATTRACTIONS

Uji is a wonderfully tranquil Kyoto daytrip. It's only 17 minutes on the rapid, or 27 on the local from Kyoto Station, but you'll feel like you're worlds away. Fans of matcha should make this trip a priority – Uji is known as the cultivator of the highest-quality green tea in Japan. Head to the banks of the river, where **Taiho-an** lets you participate in a traditional tea ceremony, hosted on the hour. If you want to get hands-on, try **Fukujuen Ujicha Kobo**, a workshop that lets you grind and prepare your own tea. **Byodo-in** is so famous it's on the back of the ¥10 coin. The vermillion structure features the famous **Phoenix Hall**, with its towering golden Buddha. Don't miss the museum, either. This dark and moody brutalist building holds a re-creation of the Phoenix Hall – birds, children and celestial entities perched on clouds float over the walls. Uji is also known for pottery. **Asahiyaki Hall** displays a range of the famous Asahiyaki pottery, made in Uji for more than 400 years. Fans of *The Tale of the Genji* will find a museum dedicated to the famous novel on Uji's right bank. A statue of author **Murasaki Shikibu** sits by Uji bridge (pictured above).

## UJI
## SHOPPING AND EATING

Coming out of the self-proclaimed 'world headquarters for tea', Uji's matcha is considered the best tea in Japan. Head down Byodo-in Omotesando dori, where you'll find tea houses and shops selling tea-related food and souvenirs. Try the matcha soft serve (pictured at left) – our favourite is at the **Masuda Tea Store**. They also do amazing tea, and their 'cappuccino stick' is actually a tea latte, which is delicious! At **Uji Hinode-in** you can 'create' your own tea flavours by mixing their ingredients. Visit amazing vintage tea store **Terashimaya Yahei Shoten** (pictured above and below) for a delicious tea set with wafers filled with rich tea cream. Marvel at old tea barrels and boxes, and the well-worn hanging lamps – especially the giant old lamp hanging over the counter. Cha dango green tea doughballs, artfully arranged in threes and skewered on sticks, are also a staple of Uji street food. If you're feeling adventurous, grab some green tea curry mix or a delicious green tea melonpan (sweet bun). This sleepy town by the river almost completely shuts down at 8pm, so grab your tea products and down as many cups as you can while the sun is still up.

**POCKET TIP**

The trip from Kyoto takes 50 minutes. Go directly to Nara on the rapid train (around ¥710) but note that it stops at Tofukuji and Uji, but not Inari.

## NARA ATTRACTIONS

Nara was the capital of Japan from 710–794. **Todai-ji** (pictured at left) is one of the seven great temples of Japan, and it's easy to see why. It's the world's largest historical wooden building, and is home to the world's largest bronze statue of Buddha. Sika deer (pictured below), a fluffy and lightly spotted variety, roam the grounds and even take the occasional wander up and down Nara's main street. They're quite friendly, especially if you happen to have a bag of the 'shika sembei' deer biscuits with you (¥150 from park vendors). At **Horyu-ji Temple** you'll find some of the world's oldest surviving wooden structures. Fans of Japanese lanterns should check out **Kasuga-taisha Shrine**, which has 3000 stone lanterns and many bronze lanterns inside. At the nearby **Kasugayama Primeval Forest**, arborists can delight in the 175 different kinds of trees and birdwatchers can watch for 60 different bird species – although identifying the 1280 species of insect could prove a challenge. Take a stroll around **Kofuku-ji** complex with its five-storey pagoda, Golden Hall and many beautiful small buildings on the temple grounds.

## NARA SHOPPING AND EATING

Nara is famous for pottery, ceramics and textiles, especially linen and wool. The shopping here is breezy, with plenty of sweets, tea and street food. The covered **Higashimuki Street** is just south of Kintetsu Nara Station, and is lined with souvenir shops, eateries and zakka (everyday items) stores. **Michidono** is a shopping arcade to the south with stores selling local ceramics, bags, and blankets made from Nara fabric. Don't miss **Naramachi Street**. Lined with original houses and shops from the Edo period, it truly evokes the spirit of how the merchants lived and worked. If you're hunting for homewares head to **Kurumi-no-ki** (pictured at left), and for local ceramics try **Five** (pictured above) and **Matsumori**. If you're after traditional crafts, pop in to **Nakagawa Masashichi Shoten**, founded in 1716. **The Nara hotel**, founded in 1909, is a famous example of Meiji-era architecture. If caffeine withdrawal is kicking in, head to new kid **Bolik Coffee**. Chic **Minamo** is also a good stop for coffee, and they do a simple lunch with local, seasonal produce. For the full fairytale experience, head deep into the east of Nara park to the primeval forest and stop for tea at thatched tea house **Mizuya-chaya** (pictured at left).

# LOCALS AND EXPERTS

### ASHLEY HORNE

Retail international services specialist

*Favourite season*

My favourite season for food is autumn. Traditionally, matching the aesthetics of the season to the foods one eats is an important aspect of Japanese cuisine. From special menus at stylish restaurants to snacks at the supermarket, if there is a sweet potato or pumpkin flavoured seasonal item, I'm going to try it!

*Favourite place to eat*

Casual and delicious, my favourite dessert shop is Karafuneya in Sanjo. With over 200 parfait varieties, you can explore Japanese flavours like matcha, kinako, red beans and sweet potato or indulge in familiar classics.

*Favourite specialty food*

Kaiseki dining is refined, subtle and harmonious. Prepared with careful attention to the seasons, shapes, flavours and textures, consuming this meal requires all the senses.

*Favourite drink*

Aodani umeshu. Cultivated near my home in the Aodani valley of Joyo, this is a sweet, aromatic plum liqueur. The plum grove is the largest in Kyoto and was praised in a poem by an ancient Japanese prince.

### MIKA TAKEO

Maker and shop owner

*Favourite season*

Spring and autumn.

*Favourite place to eat*

Cafe Chorakukan Kyoto and cafe Andante.

*Favourite specialty food*

Ramen.

*Favourite shrine*

Nishiki Tenmangu shrine (*see* p. 49). It is most beautiful at the season of autumn leaves and plum blossom in spring. On every 25th, there is a flea market of Japanese antiques and kimonos and food stalls.

*Favourite creative space*

My atelier shop Sleeping Forest (*see* p. 121) and Dreamton Village in Kameoka Kyoto. This is my favourite place to stay, very inspired, looks like Cotswolds country.

### KYLIE AND TIFFANY JOHNSON

Artisan potter (Kylie) and paper and print expert (Tiffany)

*Favourite season*

You can't beat the cherry blossoms in spring; however, a close second is the quiet of winter. If you're lucky enough to see snow falling on the garden at the Silver Pavilion it will stay with you forever.

*Favourite place to buy pottery*

A contemporary gallery in the area behind City Hall is Gallery Hitamuki. We have had arguments over who is buying what piece in this gallery.

*Favourite place to buy paper products*

Kyukyodo Honten is a stationery shop that has been around since the 1600s. It has a wonderful selection of washi papers, postcards, brushes, stamps and notebooks.

*Favourite daytrip*

A daytrip out to Shigaraki. It is a pottery village in the mountains outside of Kyoto. You can reach it by car, or train and then bus. It is one of the six old kiln towns of Japan and has many pottery shops and galleries. A visit to the I.M. Pei designed Miho Museum would also be on the list.

## GETTING TO KYOTO

### From Kansai Airport

*Train*

JR Airport Limited Express Haruka. You can use your JR Pass. Travel time is 80 minutes, ¥2850 for an unreserved seat or ¥3750 for a reserved seat.

The 'ICOCA & HARUKA' set provides a discount of an 'ICOCA' prepaid rail card with a reduced-fare ticket for the Limited Express Haruka. The ICOCA card can be used on a lot of the railways and buses in the Kansai area.

*Bus*

The Limousine Bus. Travel time 90 minutes, ¥2550.

*Additional info:*

kyotostation.com/traveling-between-kyoto-and-kansai-international-airport

*Taxi*

Book a taxi shuttle up to two days prior through MK Taxi and Yasaka Taxi. It costs between ¥3500 and ¥3600 per person and takes up to 150 minutes.

Check details on their websites: mktaxi-japan.com, www.yasaka.jp/english/shuttle

### From Tokyo

*Train*

Around 2 hours 40 minutes on the Hikari Shinkansen (with your JR Pass).

Around 2 hours 10 minutes on the superfast Nozomii Shinkansen (JR Pass cannot be used). Around ¥14,110 one way.

## KYOTO STATION INFORMATION

2F JR Kyoto Station Building, Shimogyo-ku, 3430 548
Mon–Sun, 8.30am to 7pm
Wi-fi and maps, available for free
www.jnto.go.jp/eng/spot/tic/kyoto.html

## GETTING AROUND KYOTO

### Train

If you have a Suica or Pasmo Card from Tokyo, load it up – they work here.

*Lines include:*

**JR Line** (note – these are the only trains you can use your JR Pass on).

**Kyoto subway** the Hankyu, Keihan and Eizan lines.

A one-day pass for the subway costs ¥600.

*Additional info:*

You can adjust your fare at a fare-adjustment machine when you get to your destination. http://kyoto.travel/en

### Bus

A great way to get to temples and shrines that aren't accessible via the rail lines. There are two main bus lines – the regular bus service and Raku buses, which are set up for tourism and service most of the popular sights. Raku buses are numbered 100, 101 and 102.

Check here for routes:
japanvisitor.com/japan-transport/kyoto-buses.

Board from the rear and pay into a machine at the front on exit. Pay using exact money. If you can't, there is a change machine beneath the payment slot that breaks down coins and ¥1000 notes. Flat rate is ¥220 per ride.

Buy a ¥500 all-day bus pass from convenience stores, Kyoto Station Bus Information Center, from bus drivers and at some hotels.

You can get an unlimited daily bus and subway pass for ¥1200, or ¥2000 for two days.

### Taxi

Ranks can be found outside train stations, bus terminals and larger shops. Available taxis will have illuminated signs at night. Check a sign in the corner of the front window. Free is 空車. Full is 賃走中. It will cost around ¥500–¥700 for 2 kilometres (1.2 miles), then around ¥200 for every kilometre (0.6 miles) after that. Try to be friendly – a simple hello (konnichiwa) when you enter helps. If you have an address written in Japanese, the driver can put it into their satellite navigation. There is no need to tip, but you can round up.

### Bike rental

Daily rates range from ¥500–¥2000.
You can rent bikes from Tsutaya Okazaki (TSite *see* p. 108) in North Higashiyama, j-cycle.com and konscycle.com

## MONEY

Japan's currency is the yen, denoted by ¥. It comes in denominations of ¥1000, ¥2000, ¥5000, and ¥10,000 in notes, and ¥1, ¥5, ¥10, ¥50, ¥100 and ¥500 in coins. The ¥5 and ¥50 coins have holes in the middle of them.

There is an 8 per cent consumption tax in Japan. This is sometimes included in the listed price, but often isn't, so check first. Sometimes a 'service charge' is added – for hotels and restaurants this can really stack up. Make sure you're aware of any additional costs before making a purchase.

Not all ATMs take international cards, so if you need cash, try a Seven Bank. You'll find Seven Banks in 7-Elevens and in separate outlets.

International ATMs can be found in some large stores and department stores, as well as most post offices.

## WI-FI

*Free and hotspots*

7-Eleven stores with 7Spot have free wi-fi. There are free wi-fi hotspots on Shijo dori.

To set your phone up to pick up wi-fi hotspots, follow the steps on this website: kanko.city.kyoto.lg.jp/wifi/en

*Pocket wi-fi*

Can be picked up at the airport or delivered to your hotel. There are many companies that offer pocket wi-fi, here are a couple: rentalwifi.com, japan-wireless.com
Check rates and order before you go.

*Prepaid mobile SIM card*

b-Mobile offer a great option: unlimited data for 14 days, pick up at the airport for ¥2380. See bmobile.ne.jp/english

Check rates with your provider before you leave to see if they are competitive.

## PUBLIC HOLIDAYS AND FESTIVALS

**Christmas Day** is a normal working day in Kyoto. Christmas night is considered 'date night' in Japan, especially for the young.

**New Year** is the big holiday in Japan. Celebrations involve visits to shrines to pray for good fortune and health in the coming year. Businesses can close the week before New Year, and stay shut for the first few weeks of January. Check attractions before you visit.

**Golden Week** starts on 29 April and extends into the first week of May. Book your accommodation well in advance at this time.

## SHOPPING TIPS

Carry your passport with you. That way, if you purchase something worth over ¥10,000 in major department stores or stores that have a tax-free sign, you can buy it duty-free.

Kyoto has great electronic gadgets; however, they use a different wattage and power plugs use different outlets. If you buy something, either get it converted, or buy a transformer.

## TEMPLES AND SHRINES

There are more than 17 World Heritage UNESCO sites, temples and shrines in Kyoto, and this doesn't include some of the most spectacular ones, such as Nanzen-ji or Fushimi Inari. It's easy to get overwhelmed – there are so many things to see! – so do some solid research beforehand and pick the ones that most appeal to you.

Shrines and temples are usually ruled by a specific sect or religion and can be very different. For instance, Zen temples are peaceful, atmospheric and have muted colours. They usually have beautiful gardens with raked stones and moss. Shinto shrines are more vibrant, with vermillion tori gates and buildings. They often have food stalls lining the surrounding streets.

There are also mysterious breakaway sects and deities, which can be discovered in places like Kurama-dera and Tanukidani Fudoin.

## LANGUAGE

### Pronunciation

Vowels are:

**'a'** (pronounced like the 'u' in up)

**'i'** (pronounced like the 'i' in imp)

**'u'** (pronounced as the 'oo' in book)

**'e'** (pronounced as the 'e' in egg)

**'o'** (pronounced as the 'o' in lock)

This doesn't change for any word. If two vowels are placed together, you say them as two separate, consecutive vowel sounds. Simple! The letter 'r' is pronounced as a cross between an 'r' and an 'l'; the easiest way to make this sound is to touch the roof of your mouth with the tip of your tongue.

### Useful kanji

| | |
|---|---|
| Kyoto: 京都 | Entrance: 入口 |
| Japan: 日本 | Exit: 出口 |
| Tokyo: 東京 | North: 北 |
| Yen: 円 | South: 南 |
| Male: 男 | East: 東 |
| Female: 女 | West: 西 |

Try to memorise the kanji for 'Kyoto', it's especially useful for reading the weather on television. The kanji for 'male' and 'female' are also useful for reading toilet signage in some restaurants and cafes.

### Phrase guide

**Do you speak English?** – anata wa eigo o hanashimasu ka?

**I don't understand** – wakarimasen

**I don't understand Japanese** – nihongo ga wakarimasen

**Hello** – konnichiwa

**Good morning** – ohayou gozaimasu

**Good night** – oyasuminasai

**Goodbye** – sayonara

**See you later** – mata ne

**Nice to meet you** – hajimemashite

**Please** – dozo (usually used when offering rather than asking)

**Thank you** – arigato, arigato gozaimasu

**Thank you very much** – domo arigato

**Excuse me** – sumimasen

**How are you?** – genki desu ka?

**I'm well** – genki desu or genki

**How much is this?** – ikura desu ka?

**Cheers!** – kanpai!

**I would like a beer, please** – biiru o kudasai (or add nama before biiru for a draft beer)

**Delicious** – oishii

**Can I have the bill please?** – okanjo onegaishimasu?

**It was quite a feast! (after eating a delicious meal)** – gochisousama deshita

**Taxi** – takushi

**I love Japan!** – watashi wa Nihon ga daisuki!

### Kansai language (dialect) or Kasai Ben

**Thank you** – ookin maido

**Hello** – konichiwa

**Good evening** – obandesu

**Goodbye** – sainara

**Welcome** – oideyasu

**How much?** – nambo?

**So-so** – bochi bochi

## STAYING AT A RYOKAN

A ryokan is a Japanese inn that provides one or two specially prepared meals (dinner can be served in your room in some establishments) and a bathing experience. Each guest room is decorated in traditional Japanese style, with tatami (straw) floors and a central table.

The check-in hours and meal times are strict, and some ryokans have a curfew.

Ryokans can be anywhere up to 500 years old. The experience includes sleeping in a traditional Japanese room on a futon, taking a hot springs bath, either in your room or in one of the sex-segregated baths within the ryokan (there can be both inside and outside baths).

Some ryokans now have modern rooms if you prefer to sleep in a bed. We always look for one with a private reservable bath, or one with a hot spring bath.

The price of staying in a ryokan can seem expensive, but don't forget to factor the meals into the cost.

*Recommendations*

Gion Hatanaka. Hiiragiya, Ryotei Rangetsu, Tawaraya, Togetsutei, and Ugenta.

## HOTEL RECOMMENDATIONS

*Capsule*

9 Hours Capsule Hotel

*Hostel*

Kyoto Art Hostel

Len Hostel, Cafe and Bar

Lower East 9 Hostel

*Mid-price central*

Mitsui Garden Group

*At the station*

Granvia Hotel

*Chic*

Kanra Hotel

The Screen

## CONVENIENCE STORES

You might be used to convenience stores having higher prices for junky products, but in Kyoto they are open all hours and sell great stuff, including beer, fresh fruit and veggies, sweets, magazines and delicious meals. You can even buy concert and museum tickets.

## SENTOS AND ONSENS

Onsens have water sourced from hot springs that is rich in minerals. Sentos are man-made with heated water, usually with minerals added.

Most bathhouses provide soap and shampoo for free, and towels for a small price, or you can take your own things with you. Head in and undress at the lockers, put your clothes away and walk into the shower area. Sit on the stools provided and wash yourself (and your hair if you want to) and rinse thoroughly. Once you are squeaky clean, head to the main bath and ease yourself into the water (be careful, it is usually very hot).

Take a hand towel with you if you like, but don't put it in the water. Put it at the edge of the bath or, to fit right in, put it on your head.

Most onsens don't allow you to display tattoos openly – you can cover them up with bandages.

## ETIQUETTE

Manners are very important in Japan. Always be polite. Invoke your inner sense of calm and treat everyone with respect, and respect will be returned to you.

Slip-on shoes are your friend – you will often have to take off your shoes and put them on again. Remove your shoes before stepping on a tatami (straw) mat or entering a house. Many restaurants will also require you to remove your shoes. There are usually slippers provided, but these are only for going to the bathroom. You should also take your shoes off when entering a clothing-store change room.

If you're sick with a cold, buy a face mask.

Don't take a wet umbrella into a shop; use the bags or holders provided.

## VENDING MACHINES

Vending machines are everywhere, and the variety of drinks they have is staggering. So convenient if you want a hot tea or coffee in winter, or a cold drink in summer. They can also sell anything from stationery to shirts, alcohol, oden and cup noodles.

## KYOTO FOOD

Food in Kyoto is very seasonal, and has delicacies and flavours specific to the region. Kaiseki cuisine is famous: small banquet courses of vegetables sourced from the mountains, pickled, simmered or raw. Local 'bracken' is even used in dishes. Other specialties are tofu, yuba (tofu skin), tea, noodles and unagi (eel).

Inari sushi, tofu, yuba, pickles and many types of tempura and kaiseki make Kyoto a vegan's and vegetarian's paradise, although it's always good to check for bonito flakes.

Kyoto has its own style of sushi. Mamezushi was developed for maiko (apprentice geisha) to eat, and is small, round and delicate. Regular Kyoto sushi is longer and more ornate, and features a pungent mackerel on heavily vinegared rice.

Desserts and sweets are plentiful. They are not as sweet as Western desserts, and are more intricate – they often look too beautiful to eat.

*Desserts to try include:*

**soft-serve ice-cream** – (ask for softo creamu) in amazing flavours, including soy (vegan), black sesame, matcha, cherry blossom and more

**parfaits** – piled high with sponge, matcha ice-cream, mochi balls and jelly, these towering treats are irresistible

**otabe** – rice-flour pastry with red-bean filling

**dango** – rice-flour balls on skewers

**mochi** – sweet rice cakes

**daifuku** – mochi with sweet filling

**warabi-mochi** – jelly-like sweets made from bracken starch

**wagashi** – traditional sweets made from mochi, red bean and fruit

*Tips*

Don't miss the special seasonal pleasures of kowadoko and yuka dining (*see* p. 45).

Shinkansen bentos (takeouts) in Kyoto are exceptional. If the bento packaging has a Kyoto sight on it, it's worth trying.

The first sake, tea and rice of the season are highly anticipated. Also, just about everything is pickled.

## EATING OUT

Make sure you check the opening hours of your desired cafe or restaurant. Most cafes and bars shut for one day during the week, and many cafes open around 11am or 12pm.

It's good fun to try the omakase, or chef's choice, at restaurants. The chefs decide what they think is the best choice for you.

If you don't speak Japanese, ask your hotel to make restaurant reservations on your behalf.

Most places are licensed.

Lunch starts at 11.30am and finishes between 2 and 3pm.

Set lunches are great value, especially at places that do an expensive dinner.

When using chopsticks, don't stick them upright in a bowl of rice – this is a funeral custom. Also, don't pass food to, or take food from, other people using chopsticks, and don't spear food with them (okay, we may have done this a few times …). Lastly, don't use chopsticks to move a bowl towards you.

It is customary to pour other people's drinks.

Many small eateries have plastic food models out the front of their establishment, and many cafes have pictorial menus, which is very handy if you don't speak Japanese. You can show a staff member the menu. Point to your preferred dish and say either 'onegaishimasu' (polite) or 'okudasai' – two Japanese words for 'please'.

Smoking is still allowed in some restaurants.

Tipping is not a thing in Kyoto. In fact, it will cause confusion.

## DRINKS

Sake is a big deal in Kyoto, so make sure you ask for sake specific to the region. It comes in sweet, dry and sparkling.

Craft beer is all the rage right now. Try Kuninocho, Kyoto Craft, Samurai Barley and Swan Lake. Check out Takashimaya and Iseten food halls for a full selection of drinks or head into Ichijoji Brewery, Tadg's gastro pub, Craftman, Japonica or Bungalow, who all have great selections.

## INDEX

## ABOUT THE AUTHORS

Following on from their book *Tokyo Precincts*, Michelle Mackintosh and Steve Wide bring you their take on Kyoto. They love the seasonal food (and booze), artisan crafts, machiya houses and zen gardens, and the way new generations are taking Kyoto's creative history and giving it a contemporary spin. Whenever they visit, Steve comes back with armfuls of records, books, incense and sweets, while Michelle's luggage is stuffed with boro fabrics, ceramics, books, artisan paper and vintage handcrafts.

Steve is a writer and DJ. He has toured with Primal Scream, The Prodigy, St Etienne and many more. He has presented a radio show for two decades, conducting interviews with artists such as PJ Harvey, Radiohead, and Bjork. Steve has recently released a new book on David Bowie, called *Bowie A–Z*.

Michelle is an award-winning book designer and illustrator who is equally fascinated by cuteness and refined style. She works on cookbooks, craft guides, children's picture books and young adult fiction. Michelle has written two books on analogue correspondence, *Snail Mail* and *Care Packages*. Japan is her favourite destination for design inspiration.

Together, Steve and Michelle have written six books for children. They live in Melbourne with their giant British shorthair cat, Bronte.

## ACKNOWLEDGEMENTS

Thank you so much to Melissa Kayser, Kate Armstrong, Vanessa Lanaway, Marg Bowman, Astrid Browne, Megan Ellis and Emily Maffei from Hardie Grant for all your wonderful work on *Kyoto Precincts* and for all your support along the way. Thank you to Lauren Whybrow for excellent prelim work that shaped the book.

Thank you to the wonderful Hiki Komura for helping us with translations and being the perfect company on some of our Kyoto adventures. Thank you to our lovely locals and experts Tiffany, Kylie, Ashely and Mika. Thank you Pip, Cam, Dawn, Steve and Ingrid for taking great care of Bronte while we were away. And last but by no means least, to our family and friends for all their love and support.

Thank you so much to our dear friend Tina Bouhoutsos for allowing us to use some of her truly beautiful Kyoto cherry blossom photographs.

The publisher would like to acknowledge the following people and organisations:

**Commissioning editor**
Melissa Kayser

**Managing editor**
Marg Bowman

**Project editor**
Kate J Armstrong

**Design and illustration**
Michelle Mackintosh

**Editor**
Vanessa Lanaway

**Cartography**
Emily Maffei

**Index**
Max McMaster

**Typesetting**
Megan Ellis

**Pre-press**
Megan Ellis, Splitting Image Colour Studio

**Photography credits**

All images are © Michelle Mackintosh and Steve Wide, except for the following:

Pages i, vi (2nd image, top row) & 34 Minä Perhonen; 1 Kyoto station, Vcarceler; 3, 7, 29, 33 (top image), 35 Lisn; 40–41 Matsumura, Kohei; 48 Imperial Palace, courtesy Mojamoja; 50 (top & bottom), Kyoto Design House; 87, 116, 145 (top) Shutterstock; 95 Sfera; 101, 103 (bottom image), 104 (top image), 118 (middle image), 133 (top & bottom images), 134 Shibori Museum; 145 (bottom image), 155 (bottom image) Tina Bouhoutsos; 157 (middle right), 163 (bottom) Michael Maggs; 163 (middle) Hikaru Komura; 163 (top) Kylie and Tiffany Johnson

Published in 2017 by Hardie Grant Books, a division of Hardie Grant Publishing.

Hardie Grant Books (Melbourne)
Building 1,
658 Church Street
Richmond, Victoria 3121
hardiegrantbooks.com.au

Hardie Grant Books (London)
5th & 6th Floors
52–54 Southwark Street
London SE1 1UN
hardiegrantbooks.co.uk



A Cataloguing-in-Publication entry is available from the catalogue of the National Library of Australia at www.nla.gov.au

Kyoto Pocket Precincts
9781741175172

10 9 8 7 6 5 4 3 2

Printed and bound in China by 1010 Printing International

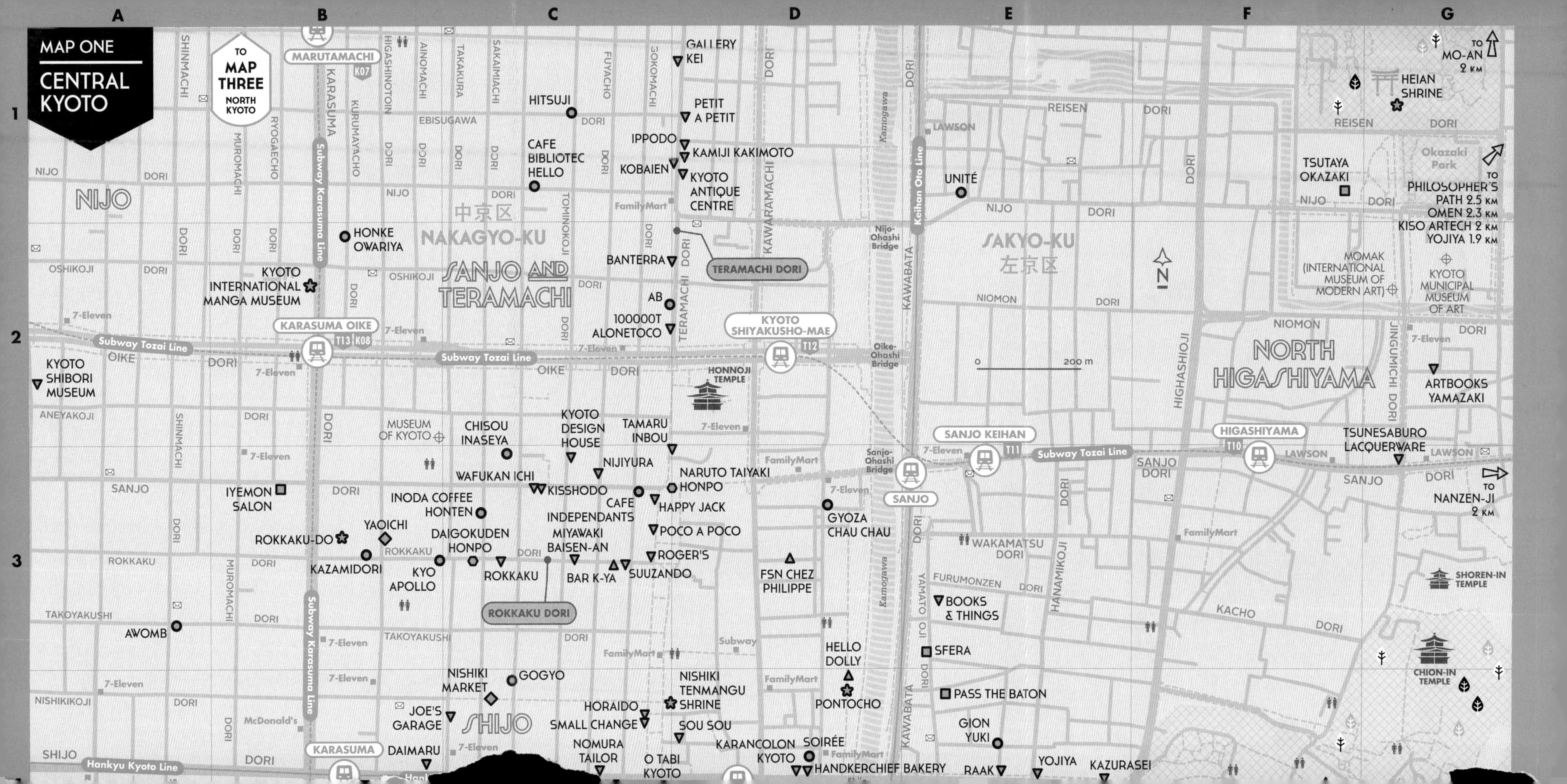
MAP ONE
CENTRAL KYOTO
TO MAP THREE NORTH KYOTO
MARUTAMACHI
K07
NIJO
SANJO AND TERAMACHI
NAKAGYO-KU
中京区
SAKYO-KU
左京区
NORTH HIGASHIYAMA
SHIJO
HITSUJI
CAFE BIBLIOTEC HELLO
GALLERY KEI
PETIT A PETIT
IPPODO
KAMIJI KAKIMOTO
KOBAIEN
KYOTO ANTIQUE CENTRE
HONKE OWARIYA
KYOTO INTERNATIONAL MANGA MUSEUM
BANTERRA
TERAMACHI DORI
AB
100000T ALONETOCO
KARASUMA OIKE
T13 K08
KYOTO SHIYAKUSHO-MAE
T12
Subway Tozai Line
Subway Karasuma Line
Keihan Oto Line
KYOTO SHIBORI MUSEUM
HONNOJI TEMPLE
Nijo-Ohashi Bridge
Oike-Ohashi Bridge
Sanjo-Ohashi Bridge
UNITÉ
LAWSON
TSUTAYA OKAZAKI
Okazaki Park
HEIAN SHRINE
TO MO-AN 2 KM
TO PHILOSOPHER'S PATH 2.5 KM
OMEN 2.3 KM
KISO ARTECH 2 KM
YOJIYA 1.9 KM
MOMAK (INTERNATIONAL MUSEUM OF MODERN ART)
KYOTO MUNICIPAL MUSEUM OF ART
ARTBOOKS YAMAZAKI
0 200 m
MUSEUM OF KYOTO
CHISOU INASEYA
KYOTO DESIGN HOUSE
TAMARU INBOU
NIJIYURA
WAFUKAN ICHI
KISSHODO
NARUTO TAIYAKI HONPO
HAPPY JACK
CAFE INDEPENDANTS
POCO A POCO
IYEMON SALON
INODA COFFEE HONTEN
YAOICHI
ROKKAKU-DO
DAIGOKUDEN HONPO
MIYAWAKI BAISEN-AN
ROGER'S
KAZAMIDORI
KYO APOLLO
ROKKAKU
BAR K-YA
SUZUANDO
ROKKAKU DORI
FSN CHEZ PHILIPPE
GYOZA CHAU CHAU
SANJO KEIHAN
T11
SANJO
HIGASHIYAMA
T10
TSUNESABURO LACQUERWARE
TO NANZEN-JI 2 KM
SHOREN-IN TEMPLE
WAKAMATSU DORI
FURUMONZEN DORI
BOOKS & THINGS
KACHO DORI
AWOMB
SFERA
HELLO DOLLY
PONTOCHO
PASS THE BATON
NISHIKI MARKET
GOGYO
NISHIKI TENMANGU SHRINE
HORAIDO
SMALL CHANGE
JOE'S GARAGE
SOU SOU
GION YUKI
CHION-IN TEMPLE
KARASUMA
DAIMARU
NOMURA TAILOR
O TABI KYOTO
KARANCOLON KYOTO
SOIRÉE
HANDKERCHIEF BAKERY
RAAK
YOJIYA
KAZURASEI
Hankyu Kyoto Line
OSHIKOJI DORI
ANEYAKOJI DORI
SANJO DORI
ROKKAKU DORI
TAKOYAKUSHI DORI
NISHIKIKOJI DORI
SHIJO DORI
OIKE DORI
REISEN DORI
NIOMON DORI
EBISUGAWA DORI
KARASUMA DORI
KAWARAMACHI DORI
KAWABATA DORI
HIGASHIOJI
HANAMIKOJI
YAMATO OJI DORI
JINGUMICHI DORI
SHINMACHI
MUROMACHI
RYOGAECHO
KURUMAYACHO
HIGASHINOTOIN
AINOMACHI
TAKAKURA
SAKAIMACHI
FUYACHO
GOKOMACHI
TOMINOKOJI
Kamogawa
7-Eleven
FamilyMart
McDonald's
Subway
N
A B C D E F G
1 2 3

cut along the dotted line

# KYOTO

A pocket guide to the city's best cultural hangouts, shops, bars and eateries

## CITY STREET MAP

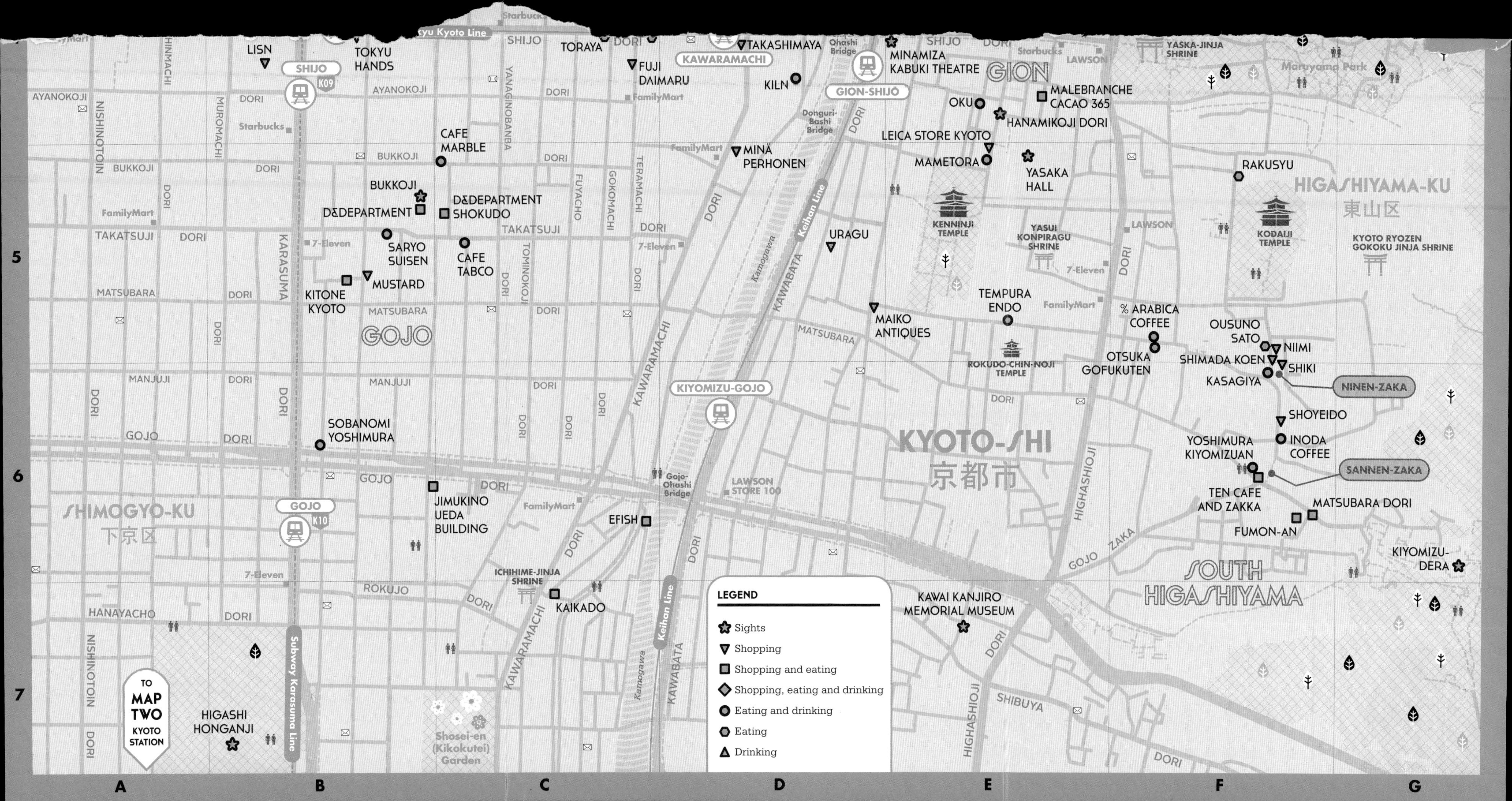
LISN
TOKYU HANDS
SHIJO
TORAYA
TAKASHIMAYA
FUJI DAIMARU
KAWARAMACHI
MINAMIZA KABUKI THEATRE
GION
YASKA-JINJA SHRINE
Maruyama Park
AYANOKOJI
KILN
GION-SHIJO
OKU
MALEBRANCHE CACAO 365
HANAMIKOJI DORI
CAFE MARBLE
BUKKOJI
MINÄ PERHONEN
LEICA STORE KYOTO
MAMETORA
YASAKA HALL
RAKUSYU
HIGASHIYAMA-KU
東山区
BUKKOJI
D&DEPARTMENT
D&DEPARTMENT SHOKUDO
KENNINJI TEMPLE
YASUI KONPIRAGU SHRINE
KODAIJI TEMPLE
KYOTO RYOZEN GOKOKU JINJA SHRINE
TAKATSUJI
SARYO SUISEN
CAFE TABCO
URAGU
KITONE KYOTO
MUSTARD
MATSUBARA
TEMPURA ENDO
% ARABICA COFFEE
GOJO
MAIKO ANTIQUES
OUSUNO SATO
NIIMI
SHIMADA KOEN
SHIKI
OTSUKA GOFUKUTEN
KASAGIYA
ROKUDO-CHIN-NOJI TEMPLE
NINEN-ZAKA
MANJUJI
KIYOMIZU-GOJO
SHOYEIDO
SOBANOMI YOSHIMURA
KYOTO-SHI
京都市
YOSHIMURA KIYOMIZUAN
INODA COFFEE
SANNEN-ZAKA
GOJO
SHIMOGYO-KU
下京区
JIMUKINO UEDA BUILDING
Gojo-Ohashi Bridge
LAWSON STORE 100
TEN CAFE AND ZAKKA
MATSUBARA DORI
EFISH
FUMON-AN
KIYOMIZU-DERA
ICHIHIME-JINJA SHRINE
KAIKADO
SOUTH HIGASHIYAMA
ROKUJO
HANAYACHO
KAWAI KANJIRO MEMORIAL MUSEUM
Keihan Line
Subway Karasuma Line
TO MAP TWO KYOTO STATION
HIGASHI HONGANJI
Shosei-en (Kikokutei) Garden
SHIBUYA
LEGEND
Sights
Shopping
Shopping and eating
Shopping, eating and drinking
Eating and drinking
Eating
Drinking
A
B
C
D
E
F
G
5
6
7

MAP THREE
NORTH KYOTO
LEGEND
Sights
Shopping
Shopping and eating
Shopping, eating and drinking
Eating and drinking
Eating
Drinking
N
0 200 m
SAKYO-KU
左京区
KITA-KU
北区
KYOTO-SHI
京都市
NORTH KYOTO
KAMIGYO-KU
上京区
NAKAGYO-KU
中京区
NIJO
Kamogawa
STARDUST
BOTANICAL GARDENS
KITAYAMA
K03
KITAOJI
K03
WIFE AND HUSBAND
Kitaoji-Bashi Bridge
Starbucks
DAISENIN TEMPLE
DAITOKUJI TEMPLE
KOTOIN TEMPLE
RYOGEN-IN TEMPLE
TO KINKAKUJI 1.7 KM
Funaoka-yama Park
KENKUN-JINJA SHRINE
KAMISOE
UMEZONO SABO
SARASA NISHIJIN
KURAMAGUCHI
K05
SHOKOKUJI TEMPLE
SENBON SHAKA-DO (DAIHO-ONJI) TEMPLE
UCHU WAGASHI
TO KITANO TENMANGU 1 KM
WAHINDO
SEIKE-YUBA
NISHIJIN TEXTILE CENTER
TO SQUIRREL AND SLEEPING FOREST 1.2 KM
IMADEGAWA
K06
IMADEGAWA DORI
TORAYA
KYOTO IMPERIAL PALACE
RAKU MUSEUM
KOTOBANOHAOTO
SONGBIRD
NIJO CASTLE
CLAMP COFFEE SARASA
COTOHA
NIJOJO-MAE
T14
NIJO
T15
MARUTAMACHI
K07
KARASUMA OIKE
T13 K08
BANBUTSUSOZOBO
Subway Karasuma Line
Subway Tozai Line
JR Sagano Line
TO MAP ONE CENTRAL KYOTO
GEN'I
OMIYA
KITAYAMA
IMAMIYA
HORIKAWA
SHINMACHI
KITA-OJI
SHIMEA
SENBON
IMADEGAWA
KARASUMA
CHEIKOIN
MARUTAMACHI
TAKEYACHO
BIFUCU
OIKE DORI
DORI
FamilyMart
7-Eleven
LAWSON
LAWSON STORE 100
Subway
1
2
3
4
5
6
7
A
B
C